The Roots of Military Doctrine

Change and Continuity in Understanding the Practice of Warfare

Dr. Aaron P. Jackson

Doctrine Desk Officer, Australian Defence Force Joint

Doctrine Centre

Visiting Fellow, Griffith Asia Institute, Griffith University

Foreword

During the 1980s a fable circulated within the US Army concerning Soviet planning for a potential war with the United States. In the most common version, a Soviet general is alleged to have declared in frustration, "It is impossible to plan against the Americans because they don't follow their own doctrine." Many readers of this book will have heard (or said) that "doctrine is only a guide." Indeed, the tactical agility demonstrated by the US Army on the battlefields of Iraq and Afghanistan is due in no small part to a cultural imperative that prizes solutions above all else.

While not disputing the value of unorthodox solutions to difficult challenges, the organizational culture that underpins this perspective has resulted in a widespread lack of knowledge of Army doctrine by company and field grade officers and mid-level and senior noncommissioned officers. Recognizing this, the Army has dramatically re-engineered its doctrine to distill the timeless principles into a series of accessible, easily read documents. This process has led to a larger discussion of what should and should not be called "doctrine," and has also included discussion of how we as members of the profession of arms conceptualize warfare. Unfortunately, this conversation has not yet included the bulk of the Army's mid-level leaders.

Dr. Jackson's monograph is an excellent contribution to remedy that shortfall. Its greatest value lies in the fact that it forces the reader to reconsider basic assumptions about the purpose and utility of doctrine, and what a nation's military doctrine says about its military institution. Jackson's arguments are well reasoned, his assertions are provocative, and his conclusions are profound. After reading this work, your view and understanding of doctrine will be powerfully enhanced, and will lead to lively discussions at every level.

Thomas E. Hanson
Colonel, Infantry
Director, Combat Studies Institute

Contents

Chapter 1

Introduction

This monograph examines military doctrine and explains why understanding its evolution and the influences that shape it are of vital importance to military practitioners, strategists, and statesmen alike. Doctrine, defined herein as the expression of a military's institutional "belief system," constitutes a significant yet hitherto unrecognized means by which this belief system can be understood and evaluated. This understanding and evaluation is in turn important because it is this belief system that determines the way a military fights, the relationship it will have with the state and society that sustain it, and its institutional culture. To get the belief system right means good strategy, victory, stable civil-military relations, and organizational wellbeing. Getting it wrong means sub-optimal strategy and operational outcomes or even defeat, strained civil-military relationships, and organizational dysfunction. This is why it is vital that military practitioners, strategists, and statesmen all have a well-developed understanding of this belief system and its implications. Yet currently, many do so only subconsciously, if at all. The aim of this monograph is to help make this understanding explicit.

The potentially detrimental results of many military practitioners, strategists, and statesmen having developed only an implicit understanding of the military belief system can be seen in the state of conceptual confusion that has reigned since the end of the Cold War. Today, Western militaries are awash with competing and contrasting terms, ideas, and concepts. As Colin S. Gray recently observed, "Americans in the 2000s went to war and by and large have remained conceptually wounded."[1] Brian McAllister Linn traced the roots of this problem even further back asserting that "even before the [Global War on Terror] the defense community was in the midst of a vibrant debate over whether the nature of war itself had changed."[2]

This conceptual confusion is most prominently manifest in the volume of buzzwords and imprecise terms that have been coined in recent decades to describe the nature of warfare and ways that it should be prosecuted. Linn, for example, has charged that "the Pentagon routinely issues directives purporting to give a concept of war that are little more than gibberish."[3] The problem is by no means limited to the US military. In a critique of the Israeli Defense Force's (IDF) performance in the 2006 conflict in Lebanon, Milan Vego wrote, "New terms such as *strategic directive, strategic purpose, system boundary, operational boundaries, campaign organizing theme*, and *rival system rationale* were overused in place of traditional military terms. Units were ordered to 'render the enemy incoherent,' make the enemy feel 'distress' or 'chased down,' or 'achieve standoff domination of the theatre.'"[4] In short, contemporary western militaries are facing a conceptual crisis brought on by an even deeper uncertainty about the nature of the strategic and operational environments and the links between them, and indeed, whether or not it is still appropriate to delineate between them.

To address this conceptual crisis as well as to address or avert other potentially detrimental results of the failure to develop an explicit understanding of the military belief system, it is necessary to address the underlying cause of this failure. This requires going to the heart of what a military institutionally (and by inference what the community of practitioners that constitute it) believes and making these beliefs explicitly known. What is a legitimate understanding of the military's role considered to be and what is considered illegitimate? And why is that the case? Only once these questions are answered can the cause of the conceptual crisis be understood and only then can it be properly addressed. Making knowledge of a military's institutional belief system explicit is vital because this system needs to be founded upon a robust intellectual construct to ensure that strategic, operational, and tactical analysis is sound. If this intellectual construct is not robust, buzzwords will continue to proliferate but performance will nonetheless falter.

This monograph examines the evolution and nature of the belief systems of western militaries through an analysis of their military doctrine. More specifically, it examines the meaning and significance of the ways in which English speaking western militaries conceptualize, develop, implement, and reform their doctrine.[5] This analysis is significant because, as mentioned above and elaborated below, doctrine constitutes the most visible expression of a military's "belief system." Doctrine therefore provides a means to gauge the state of a military's institutional thought and the evolution of this thought over time.

In undertaking its analysis, this monograph chronicles the evolution of military doctrine since the 17th century. It employs ontology and epistemology as the key tools for its analysis even though in military circles these are not commonly used terms (Robert Leonhard, for example, remarked that "as a professional infantry officer, when I first heard the word *epistemology*, I thought it had something to do with field sanitation!").[6] But, adhering to Confucius' adage that "the beginning of wisdom is calling things by their right names," these terms are used herein because they are the right names for what is under discussion.[7] In essence, ontology is the study of the nature of reality and the relationships between objects within it and epistemology is the theory of knowledge acquisition. To illustrate the significance of these terms with a simple example, an ontology is the division of military operations into the categories "humanitarian," "peace enforcement," "counterinsurgency" and "conventional war." Epistemology is the cognitive process used when evaluating a military operation and assigning it to one of the categories. A more detailed explanation of the meaning of both terms is given below.

This monograph posits that a military's understanding of its relationship with the state and society that sustains it has influenced doctrine to a much greater degree than has been acknowledged in almost all of the existing literature about doctrine development. Reaching an explicit comprehension of the ontology and epistemology of military doctrine is vital to enabling military practitioners, strategists, statesmen, and even doctrine writers, to undertake a more thorough evaluation of the nature and content of military doctrine and to ensure that the institutional belief system it represents is founded upon a robust intellectual construct. This will lead to better evaluations of the strategic and operational concepts that appear in doctrine, which in turn will contribute to enhanced military strategy development and ultimately, to better military performance.

Structure

This monograph proceeds in six chapters, this being the first. In the next section of this chapter key terms are defined including military doctrine, epistemology and ontology, and their interrelationships are also examined.

The second chapter offers a history of military doctrine from its emergence in the early 17th century to the end of the 20th. This discussion is undertaken from an ontological perspective and it is determined that doctrinal ontology can be divided into four "schools," each of which emerged at a different point in doctrinal history. These schools are labeled the technical manual, tactical manual, operational manual, and military strategic manual schools, with the delineation between each school being determined by three factors. First, the scope of the content and intended audience broadens between each school. Second, the manner in which manuals in each school is applied varies with manuals in each successive school being applied respectively as instruction manuals, training aids, guidance, and as instruments for analysis. Third, each manual has a different type of relationship to a military's accepted institutional ontology.

This relationship can be described as absent (technical manual school), implicit (tactical manual school), explicit (operational manual school), and inquisitive (military strategic school), by which it is meant that manuals in the fourth school are used as a means to examine ontological questions and pose answers to those questions.

In the third chapter, the relationship between these schools is analyzed from training and educational, scientific and bureaucratic perspectives. These perspectives are adopted because each sheds light on a different aspect of the military's institutional belief system as it is expressed within doctrine and together these perspectives also explore the range and significance of the relationships between doctrine, strategy, the military, and its environment. It is also determined in this chapter that despite the differences between each of the four ontological schools, doctrine has nevertheless consistently employed ontological **realism** as the basis of its discourse. This has formed an enduring bond between each of the schools of doctrinal ontology and has usually ensured that they remain mutually compatible despite the different scope of their focus.

Turning next to the epistemology of doctrine, the fourth chapter determines that **positivism**, an approach characterized by (self-proclaimed) rationality and objectivity, has provided the epistemological foundation of doctrine for the first four hundred years of its existence. As such, examples of positivist approaches abound within doctrine and include most measurable, quantifiable, or linear processes such as that used to determine when a soldier has qualified on a weapon system or even the military planning process itself.

While positivism remains dominant, since the start of the 21st century **anti-positivism**, emphasizing relativity and subjectivity, has begun to influence doctrine, signaling what is perhaps the most salient change in the nature of doctrine since its inception. The emergence of this new epistemological approach and the state of the debate surrounding its most prominent manifestation to date (that being the "design" concept featured in several recent US Army, Marine Corps and joint doctrine manuals) is also addressed in the fourth chapter.[8]

The fifth chapter considers the significance and implications of doctrinal ontology and epistemology with discussion focusing especially on the likely direction in which anti-positivist doctrine will evolve in the near future. It is asserted that the shift from positivism to anti-positivism is arguably the most pervasive paradigm shift to have occurred in 400 years of doctrinal history.[9] Although several issues are identified that need to be resolved before this shift is complete, appreciating its potential implications for the conduct of military affairs is already of paramount importance to military practitioners, strategists, statesmen, and doctrine writers alike. Anti-positivist approaches have the potential to alter the way in which militaries perceive their relationships with external organizations including other government agencies, allied militaries, enemies, and even the state itself and doctrine itself has potential to enable other organizations to better communicate with militaries. Finally, developing a better understanding of the ontology and epistemology underlying terms, concepts, and ideas has the potential to enable doctrine writers to better thresh the wheat from the chaff.

The idea of doctrine as a belief system is revisited in the conclusion (Chapter 6) and the monograph's core argument—that developing an explicit comprehension of the ontology and epistemology of military doctrine will assist military practitioners, strategists, statesmen, and doctrine writers to ensure that the institutional belief system doctrine represents is founded upon a robust intellectual construct—is elaborated. This is of the utmost importance because a robust appropriate institutional belief system (and the doctrine that represents it) contributes greatly to determining whether a military will succeed or fail at implementing national strategy and strategic policy, at developing corresponding military strategy, and at conducting military operations.

Before proceeding, it is pertinent to note that this monograph's focus is limited to the doctrine produced by English speaking militaries. Other militaries are discussed but only in instances where their doctrine has subsequently had a substantial impact within their English speaking counterparts. In the words of Azar Gat, "the center of military thought has normally tended to follow the center of military power."[10] For this reason, the discussion in this monograph of developments during the 17th to the 19th centuries is necessarily Euro-centric, while discussion of the 20th and 21st centuries, shifts its focus to North America, in particular to the United States. Despite its limited focus, this study nonetheless has the potential to serve as the base for the future conduct of a broader cross-cultural examination of other militaries, as the ontological and epistemological approaches it details provide a mechanism for this to occur.

Key Terms

The first problem encountered when attempting a study of military doctrine is definitional. Specifically, the term "doctrine" has been defined in so many ways that it has become thoroughly ill-defined.[11] For example, doctrine has been described as "what is written down, usually at the highest levels, for dissemination throughout an army, the usual intention being therefore to instruct and standardize."[12] It has been determined that it "stands for an institutional culture of conceptual thinking on the nature of conflict and the best conduct of warfare"[13] and it has been observed that it "is regarded as the foundation of military professional knowledge. Doctrine is to soldiers what blueprints are to architects or briefs to lawyers."[14]

Official definitions of doctrine do not offer any additional clarity. The United States Department of Defense (DoD) *Dictionary of Military and Associated Terms*, for example, defines doctrine as "fundamental principles by which the military forces or elements thereof guide their actions in support of national objectives." To this very general definition the seemingly paradoxical clarification is added that, "it is authoritative but requires judgment in application."[15]

This monograph embraces a definition of doctrine that differs from all of those given above yet does not dispute the accuracy of any. Simply, it is determined herein that doctrine is representative of a "belief system."[16]

More precisely, it is posited that doctrine is the most visible expression of a military's belief system. Primarily, this belief system regards the accepted paradigms by which a military understands, prepares for, and (at least in theory) conducts warfare. Significantly, such paradigms are important corollaries of the perceptions a military has of its institutional role and legitimacy within broader society. Hence, at a greater level of abstraction, doctrine also reflects this aspect of a military's belief system. Importantly, both of these aspects of the belief systems of western militaries' have evolved over time, and as a result, so too has the nature of doctrine.

Notwithstanding this definition, three caveats apply to the discussion undertaken herein. First, doctrine is considered to be expressive of an **institutional** belief system that may not necessarily align with the belief system of all or even a substantial minority of the individuals that are a part of that institution. For this reason, the military writings of individual scholars from Sun Tzu to the modern era are not considered to be doctrinal until they have been formally accepted as such by a military institution.[17] Second, doctrine, at least as it is conceived today, takes the form of written manuals.[18] Although this has not always been the case—the original understanding of doctrine is simply "teaching, body of teachings, or learning,"[19] and for much of their histories, western militaries have employed oral rather than written conceptualizations of doctrine—analysis herein is concerned primarily with doctrine in its written form.

Third, there is general acceptance (often implicitly) that doctrine is essentially cognitive in nature. The sources quoted in the opening paragraph of this section all hint at this aspect and it is also central to the definition of doctrine embraced herein. As Dennis Drew and Donald Snow observe, "the use of the word **believe** [in the definition of doctrine] suggests that doctrine is the result of an examination and interpretation of the available evidence."[20] Both examination and interpretation are cognitive actions, as cognition itself is "the mental action or process of acquiring knowledge and understanding through thought, experience, and the senses."[21] Doctrine and the belief system it represents are therefore, the result of a process of knowledge acquisition and development.

Because epistemology is concerned primarily with knowledge acquisition and development, doctrine is understood to play an inherently epistemological role within the military institutions that produce it. Discussion herein is thus unavoidably epistemological also, and the term warrants further explanation. As an academic discipline, epistemology is the branch of philosophy that examines theories of knowledge.[22] It "explores and illuminates the origins, nature, methods, and limits of human thought, perception, knowledge, understanding, and learning."[23] It is also concerned with identifying the assumptions made, either explicitly or implicitly, when one attempts to come to an understanding of something. The methods by which humans acquire knowledge has also been a focus of epistemological research, as are mechanisms used for the demarcation of "true" from "false" knowledge.[24]

This is important because "everyone adheres to some theory about what constitutes warranted knowledge—a set of epistemological commitments which provide us with criteria for distinguishing between reliable and unreliable knowledge."[25] Military practitioners, strategists, statesmen, and doctrine writers are no exception. In the case of doctrine, its very nature as well as its role in legitimizing (or delegitimizing) military strategies, theories, and concepts is epistemological. For example, the inclusion within doctrine of a concept purporting to explain the nature of warfare implies that this concept has been accepted as valid by the military as an institution. The decision making process leading to this acceptance, whether undertaken consciously through deliberate evaluation or unconsciously through instinct is an epistemological process. Closely related to epistemology is ontology, which examines the nature of being and the first principles—or categories—involved. Epistemology is concerned with the manner by which humans acquire knowledge whereas ontology is concerned with the formulation of taxonomies that enable one to reach an understanding of relationships between entities.[26] Although doctrine itself is epistemological, the theories and concepts that are legitimized or delegitimized by their inclusion within or omission from doctrine, encapsulate a military's accepted and rejected ontological approaches to understanding, preparing for, and (supposedly) prosecuting warfare.

To extend the simple example offered in the opening pages of this monograph, delineating "irregular" from "conventional" warfare is ontological as it involves the construction of a taxonomy that enables the categorization of military activities. Evaluating a war in order to determine whether the war is irregular or conventional is epistemological, as the process of evaluation involves making intellectual assumptions in order to reach an understanding of the entity under study (in this instance the war in question). In the case of a doctrine manual, the inclusion of a discussion asserting that there is a difference between irregular and conventional warfare indicates the manual's ontology. The cognitive process used during the development of the manual to evaluate this ontology and determine that it is acceptable for inclusion within the doctrine indicates the epistemology underlying the manual.

While at first glance this seems to imply a hierarchical relationship, epistemology and ontology are actually interrelated, meaning that they continually shape one another. To illustrate this by continuing the above example, let's suppose that a military determines (using an epistemological process) that it is best to produce two separate doctrine manuals, one discussing military strategies for winning irregular warfare and the other military strategies for winning conventional warfare. In this case, the ontological model adopted will in turn influence the subsequent epistemological process that determines exactly what type of strategy will be established within each of the two manuals.

A simple, "real-world" example of the overlapping nature of ontological and epistemological processes is US Marine Corps General James Mattis' well-known memorandum ordering US Joint Forces Command to cease using the term "effects based operations." In declaring that "a clear understanding of [this] concept has proven problematic and elusive for US and multinational personnel," Mattis showed that he considered—although it is unlikely that he did so in these terms—that the concept's ontology was not sound and that its implementation did not align with the epistemological processes that he as a military practitioner considered warranted.[27]

Notes

1. Colin S. Gray, "Concept Failure: COIN, Counterinsurgency, and Strategic Theory," *Prism*, Vol. 3, No. 3, June 2012, pp. 18-19.

2. Brian McAllister Linn, *The Echo of Battle: The Army's Way of War,* Cambridge, MA: Harvard University Press, 2007, pp. 1-2.

3. Linn, *The Echo of Battle*, p. 3.

4. Milan N. Vego, "A Case Against Systemic Operational Design," *Joint Force Quarterly*, No. 53, 2nd Quarter 2009, p. 73.

5. Unless stated otherwise, hereinafter the term "doctrine" is used exclusively in reference to military doctrine.

6. Robert R. Leonhard, *The Principles of War for the Information Age,* Novato, CA: Presidio, 1998, p. 264.

7. Quoted in: Charles M. Westenhoff, *Military Airpower: A Revised Digest of Airpower Opinions and Thoughts,* Maxwell Air Force Base: Air University Press, 2007, p. 239.

8. These manuals include: Headquarters, Department of the Army, FM 5-0 *The Operations Process,* Washington, DC: U.S. Government Printing Office, March 2010; Headquarters, U.S. Marine Corps, MCWP 5-1 *Marine Corps Planning Process,* Washington, DC: U.S. Government Printing Office, 24 August 2010; Joint Chiefs of Staff, U.S. Department of Defense, JP 5-0 *Joint Operation Planning,* Washington, DC: U.S. Government Printing Office, August 11, 2011.

9. "Paradigm shift" is used here in the Kuhnsian sense. The term's meaning and significance will be elaborated in the fifth chapter.

10. Azar Gat, *A History of Military Thought: From the Enlightenment to the Cold War,* Oxford: Oxford University Press, 2001, Book I, p. 107.

11. Dennis Drew and Donald Snow assert that "doctrine is an ill-defined, poorly understood, and often confusing subject." Dennis M. Drew & Donald M. Snow, *Making Strategy: An Introduction to National Security Processes and Problems*, Maxwell Air Force Base: Air University Press, 1988, p. 163.

12. Paul Johnston, "Doctrine is not Enough: The Effect of Doctrine on the Behavior of Armies," *Parameters*, Vol. XXX, No. 3, Autumn 2000, p. 30.

13. Markus Mäder, *In Pursuit of Conceptual Excellence: The Evolution of British Military-Strategic Doctrine in the Post-Cold War Era, 1989-2002,* Studies in Contemporary History and Security Policy No. 13, Bern: Peter Lang, 2004, p. 22.

14. Michael Evans, *Forward from the Past: The Development of Australian Army Doctrine, 1972 – Present*, Study Paper No. 301, Canberra: Australian Army Land Warfare Studies Centre, August 1999, p. 2.

15. The epistemological implications of this clarification will be revisited in the fourth chapter of this monograph. Joint Chiefs of Staff, U.S. Department of Defense, Joint Publication (JP) 1-02, *Department of Defense Dictionary of Military and Associated Terms,* as amended through August 2009, p. 171. This is closely aligned to the North Atlantic Treaty Organization (NATO) definition of doctrine, as well as to the definition used by several other English-speaking militaries. NATO, *NATO-Russia Glossary of Contemporary Political and Military Terms,* Brussels: NATO-Russia Joint Editorial Working Group, undated but promulgated online on June 8, 2001, p. 77. Available from *www.nato.int/docu/ glossary/eng/index.htm,* accessed on December 20, 2008.

16. Drew & Snow, *Making Strategy,* p. 163, define doctrine as "what we believe about the best way to conduct military affairs." This is the closest definition to that used in this monograph, and I am indebted to Howard Coombs for suggesting the term used herein.

17. Brian Holden-Reid, *A Doctrinal Perspective: 1988-98,* Occasional Paper No. 33, United Kingdom: Strategic and Combat Studies Institute, May 1998, p. 13.

18. Johnston, "Doctrine is not Enough," p. 30.

19. Catherine Soanes & Angus Stevenson, eds., *Oxford Dictionary of English,* 2nd ed., Oxford: Oxford University Press, 2003, p. 511.

20. Drew & Snow, *Making Strategy,* p. 163. Original emphasis.

21. Soanes & Stevenson, eds., *Oxford Dictionary of English,* 2nd ed., p. 335.

22. Michael Williams, *Problems of Knowledge: A Critical Introduction to Epistemology,* Oxford: Oxford University Press, 2001, p. 1.

23. Richard Maltz, "The Epistemology of Strategy", paper presented at the XX Annual Strategy Conference, U.S. Army War College, Carlisle PA, April 17, 2009, 2.

24. Gibson Burrell & Gareth Morgan, *Sociological Paradigms and Organisational Analysis: Elements of the Sociology of Corporate Life,* Portsmouth: Heinemenn, 1979, pp. 1-2.

25. Phil Johnson & Joanne Duberley, *Understanding Management Research: An Introduction to Epistemology,* London: Sage Publications, 2000, p. 5.

26. Burrell & Morgan, *Sociological Paradigms and Organisational Analysis,* pp. 1-4.

27. General J. N. Mattis, *U.S. Joint Forces Command Commander's Guidance for Effects Based Operations,* unpublished memorandum dated 14 August 2008, quote p. 3.

Chapter 2

The Four "Schools" of Doctrinal Ontology

This chapter offers a reconsideration of the history of written military doctrine. Its discussion proceeds chronologically but ontology is used as its principle analytical tool (doctrinal epistemology is discussed in later chapters). Through this history, it is determined that doctrine manuals can be grouped into four "schools," which can be labeled the technical manual, tactical manual, operational manual and military strategic manual schools.

In addition to each school having emerged at a different point in time and as a result of different events, there are three noticeable distinctions between the schools. First is the nature of their relationship to a military's ontology. Doctrine in the technical manual school has no relationship to a military's ontology, as manuals in this school discuss matters at a micro scale without discussing how these connect to other matters (an instruction manual for the employment of a weapon system is a typical example of this doctrine). Tactical manuals have an implicit relationship with ontology as they assume away "bigger picture" aspects of military endeavor in order to concentrate on events within a localized time and space (such as the "battlefield").

Operational manuals have an explicit relationship with a military's ontology as they define preferred methods of conducting military activities but their scope is nevertheless limited, although they may detail the relationship a military has with the state and the types of operations it expects to undertake, they give these details as though they are a constant and usually do so only to the extent necessary in order to explain why particular operating methods have been established. Military strategic manuals take their discussion a step further, constituting a means by which militaries examine a broad range of ontological questions and pose answers to them. In addition to proffering an approach to strategic or operational conduct that is likely to overcome the challenges posed within a given environment, they also actively seek to define the nature of these challenges and to determine what the environment itself is and, in some cases, why it is.

The second noticeable distinction between the four schools is that the scope of the contents and the intended audience broadens between each school. At one end of the spectrum, technical manuals are usually aimed at users of specific systems within segments of the military while at the other end, military strategic manuals are usually aimed at broad internal (military) and external audiences. The final distinction is that the manner in which the manuals in each school are applied varies with manuals in each successive school being applied respectively as instruction manuals, training aids, guidance, and as instruments for analysis.

The Technical Manual School

The written doctrine of Western militaries has a lineage dating to 1607 when "the first modern drill book" was published. The book, *Wapenhandlingen van Roers, Musqetten, Ende Spiessen* [*Arms Drill with Arquebus, Musket, and Pike*], contained—in the form of a series of sketches—instructions for the correct employment of the modern weapon systems of its day. Its publication in Amsterdam the year after the establishment of the first modern Military Training Academy at Sedan in northern France is a noteworthy coincidence.[1]

Both of these events coincided with the transition, heralded as a "revolution" by some,[2] of warfare into what has been labeled its "modern" form. The key military reforms that characterized this transition were the universal introduction of gunpowder weapons within European militaries and the widespread establishment of permanent military forces within European states.[3] Importantly this military transition was accompanied by, and indeed was a significant part of, a series of broader changes within Western European society. Most notable among these was the emergence of the modern state system itself, which has often been viewed as a consequence of the signing of the Treaties of Münster and Osnabrück in 1648. By the end of the 17th century this transformation had led to the establishment of military academies in many European states and to the publication of numerous drill manuals.[5]

Since these early drill manuals were not official publications of the emergent military institutions of the period, they cannot be considered as doctrine at least not as it is defined herein.[6] Despite this, they are nonetheless the forebears of what has since become the first of four distinctly recognizable "schools" of doctrinal ontology. This first school, which could be labeled the "technical manual" school, is characterized by doctrine that provides concise instructions about how to employ various military systems, usually hardware. Doctrine manuals that fit into this category are generally narrow in focus, are usually employed as "instruction manuals", and tend to clearly delineate correct from incorrect processes and procedures in absolute and inflexible terms.

Although doctrine that fits within the technical manual school is almost always "micro" in focus, it occasionally transcends this focus and has a "macro" effect. The US Army's "training revolution" of the early 1970s is a good example:

> [General Paul M.] Gorman formed a joint army-academic analysis group and instructed them to identify and list all the steps necessary to accomplish a particular task or mission in the most efficient manner. They then distributed these lists in the form of training manuals mandating exactly how each task was to be performed. An annual evaluation is the final step in the process, requiring soldiers and units to demonstrate their mastery of these "skill sets."[7]

In this case, the combined effect of several doctrine manuals enabled them to have a greater collective impact than the sum of their parts.[8]

From an ontological perspective, what is omitted from the doctrine that constitutes this school is arguably more significant than what is included. Absent from this doctrine is anything that addresses the possible impact of the environment external to the system under discussion. A technical manual tells a soldier how to **use** his weapon; it does not give any information about when it is appropriate to do so. Because it omits this information, doctrine in the first school fails to even implicitly consider a military's ontology. This may explain why some definitions of doctrine have deliberately excluded this school and why acceptance of this exclusion has gradually increased as the other schools of written doctrine have emerged.[9]

Hypothetically, if this school of doctrine existed in a proverbial vacuum, or in other words if it was representative of the entire extent of a military's belief system, that belief system would be characterized by the existence of only a singular, narrow, process-focused outlook. The hypothetical military in question would be incapable of undertaking anything other than pre-determined tasks in adherence with a prescribed sequence. Clearly, this approach to the conduct of warfare is utterly impractical. Soldiers have always needed to know both how **and** when to use their weapons. As a result this school of doctrine has never existed exclusively, although it has often been the only doctrine that is written down.

In the absence of other schools of written doctrine what has instead existed beyond technical manuals has generally been transient, informal, and highly personalized. Doctrine of this nature has been identified historically within the British Army:

> Largely eschewing formal written doctrine, the Army made a cult of pragmatism, flexibility, and an empirical approach...That is not to say that the British Army entirely neglected "doctrine" broadly defined...However, doctrine tended to be semi-formal at best was centered around one individual commander or existed in a specific set of circumstances (usually high-intensity war) and was not necessarily easily transferrable elsewhere; and in some cases it was more honored in the breach than the observance.[10]

The existence of unwritten doctrine of a similar nature has also been identified within the US and several Commonwealth Navies as well as within the US and Canadian air forces right up until the latter part of the 20th century.[11] In all of these militaries, as well as in several others, champions of this form of doctrine have cited its flexibility as its key strength and opponents have attacked the erratic success rate that has resulted from its reliance on the abilities of individual commanders.[12]

In the century and a half from the signing of the Treaties of Münster and Osnabrück in 1648 to the commencement of the French Revolutionary Wars in 1792, the technology used to prosecute warfare advanced steadily if incrementally. Wars occurred for several reasons, sometimes yielding decisive results and other times not.[13] Although doctrine also developed incrementally, a few important factors resulted in the ongoing primacy of unwritten doctrine throughout this period. One of these factors was the common attitude to war:

> To the extent that broad publics thought about problems of war and peace, they were generally resigned to war as a fixed characteristic of human life or as a divine punishment for the sins of people. War was taken for granted. Causes and consequences were not the object of study or speculation. Writers were more interested in the details of diplomatic maneuvers and military campaigns.[14]

Another factor was the similarities between the social structures within militaries and the societies that sustained them:

> The expanded armed forces of the period developed in a fashion that did not challenge the social reality of societies organized around the principles of inegalitarianism and inheritance. Larger armies brought more opportunities to nobles who benefited

both from the assumption that they were naturally suited for positions of command and from the fact that this was usually the case. Thus, armies were not forces "outside" society but rather reflections of patterns of social control and influence and the beliefs that gave cohesion to them.[15]

Throughout this period, the belief was commonplace that effective military command, defined as the successful formulation and execution of strategy, was an inherent trait possessed exclusively by the nobility. Command appointments were thus reserved for the nobility except in the most unusual of circumstances.[16] This perception also appears to have been fundamental in perpetuating the primacy of unwritten doctrine throughout this period, despite the promulgation of a limited number of written doctrine manuals, most of which fit exclusively within the first school.

The Tactical Manual School

Despite the ongoing primacy of unwritten doctrine, accompanied by a limited number of manuals that fit within the first school of written doctrine, the 18th century nevertheless witnessed the production of the first theoretical treatises that aligned with the second school. During the latter part of the 18th century in particular, several military theorists offered treatises that pre-empted the development of the second school. Most notably, these theorists included Paul Gideon Joly de Maizeroy and Jacques Antoine Hippolyte Comte de Guibert in France, Henry Humphrey Evans Lloyd in Britain, and Adam Heinrich Dietrich von Bürlow in Prussia. Together with a few others, these writers began to theorize about tactics mostly using a mixture of historical studies of early-to-mid-18th century warfare and Roman warfare and the application of geometry as their methodology. [17] In line with the definition of doctrine used in this study, their works are personal rather than institutional, and therefore cannot be considered as **doctrine.** However, they nonetheless laid the foundation for the emergence of the second school of doctrine in the late 18th century and its proliferation in the 19th.

This emergence was gradual, beginning in what was at the time considered within Europe to be a military backwater – the United States. Specifically, in 1779 the newly-raised US Army published *Regulations for the Order and Discipline of the Troops of the United States, Part 1.* This manual prescribed and thereby standardized tactical drill within the US Army and having been approved by (then) Major General George Washington as well as by Congress prior to its publication and distribution throughout the Army, it also constitutes one of the first examples of an "official" doctrine manual.[18] Owing to its focus on tactical **drill**, this manual had much in common with first school doctrine manuals. However, its discussion of tactics also aligned it with the second school and it can therefore be viewed as something of a "bridging" document between these schools.

Within European militaries, the second distinctive school of written doctrinal ontology emerged during the 19th century. This emergence was gradual, as was the proliferation of this type of doctrine amongst Europe's professional militaries:

> [N]either Wellington nor Napoleon had doctrinal manuals describing for them the principles of war and the approach they should take towards operations. However, even while Napoleon was still campaigning, the famous Swiss military commentator Baron Henri Jomini began publishing works purporting to explain Napoleon's method...As militaries professionalized and standardized (and bureaucratized), there came about an increasing tendency to formalize not just the tactical details of drill but the very approach to war that higher commanders should take...by 1914 this approach was quite formally established in all major Western forces to a greater or lesser extent.[19]

Importantly, the French Revolutionary and subsequent Napoleonic Wars, which together ran from 1792 to 1815, marked a significant transformation in the nature of European warfare.[20] This transformation was the catalyst for the emergence of a new school of doctrinal ontology within European militaries.

Just as they triggered drastic reforms to the social structure of several European states, so too did the French Revolutionary and Napoleonic Wars bring about a change in common attitudes towards and the prosecution of warfare.[21] For doctrine development, a key change was the growth in the professionalism of the officer corps of European militaries. Beginning in France following the Revolution and spreading through other European states during the 19th century, old systems of commissioning officers according to social status and societal position were gradually replaced by selection based increasingly on merit.[22] With this increase in military professionalism came an increased interest amongst military officers in the study of warfare. Thus, the post-Napoleonic period witnessed an acute acceleration of a trend that had begun during the latter part of the 18th century when the impact of the Enlightenment on military thought had brought about an expansion in the role of military academies and colleges.[23]

The second school of written doctrinal ontology emerged against this backdrop and its proliferation was a product of these and other military reforms of the 19th century. This school could be labeled the "tactical manual" school. Manuals in this school purport to describe the most up-to-date tactics at the time of their publication and several were initially based on the tactics developed by Napoleon, as described by the key military thinkers of the late 18th and early 19th centuries, Jomini the most famous amongst them.[24]

Similarly to the technical manual school, manuals in the tactical manual school were initially published externally to militaries although several manuals were tacitly selected to become doctrine through their semi-official use as instruction manuals at military colleges. By the turn of the 20th century however, several militaries had begun to formally publish tactical manuals for official use and it is at about this time that these manuals became "doctrine" in a form that would be easily recognizable today.[25]

Amongst the new tactical manuals formally published by Western militaries in the early 20th century was the US Army's 1905 *Field Service Regulations*, the forerunner to Field Manual (FM) 3-0 *Operations*. This manual was clearly situated within the tactical manual school of doctrinal ontology and it has been observed that it, as well as subsequent editions, "was written at—and reflected only—the tactical level right down to the advent of AirLand Battle doctrine in the early 1980s."[26] For example, the 1941 edition, which established an intellectual foundation for the Army's success in the Second World War,[27] contained very specific "doctrines of leading troops in combat and tactics of the combined arms." The intent of these "doctrines" was to constitute "the basis of instruction of all arms and services for field service."[28]

This is indicative of both the intent and limitations of the content of doctrine in the tactical manual school. This doctrine has tended to be applied as a "training aid" during courses at military academies and colleges and during major exercises where it assists students to develop workable solutions to tactical problems. Unlike the technical procedures described by manuals in the first school, there is scope for flexibility in the application of doctrine in this school even though it ultimately serves to delineate acceptable from unacceptable tactical practice. Although doctrine of this nature has long expounded (supposedly immutable) "principles of war," it remains limited in scope because of its otherwise exclusively tactical focus.[29] Thus it is of little use to higher commanders seeking to successfully maneuver larger forces between tactical encounters and, as a result of this limitation, it has generally been accompanied by the continued existence of unwritten doctrine.

Furthermore, its limited scope means that the ontological assumptions underlying doctrine in the tactical manual school are implicit. Answers to ontological questions that might be raised about the relationship between militaries and the states and societies in which they exist, the nature of the international environment in which they operate, the role that they play within that environment, and their development of military strategy, are all taken for granted. Having assumed away the answers to questions about these subjects, tactical manuals are free to concentrate instead on developing approaches to overcoming an enemy on the battlefield.

In the US Army this concentration led to the development of what has since been labeled the "American Way of War" (or as Antulio Echevarria has suggested, what might be more accurately called the "American Way of Battle").[30] This so-called way of war focuses primarily on overcoming manpower shortages by exploiting new technologies to tactically attrit the enemy on the battlefield. [31] In so doing, it assumes away its own inherent ontology, unquestioningly embracing a view of warfare in which it is assumed that first, there will be a battlefield and second, that the outcome of a battle (or a series of battles) is the most important factor in determining the outcome of a war. Of course, ontological assumptions of this nature have not been limited to the US Army. John Ellis for example, identified the existence of similar ontological assumptions on the part of several First World War European militaries (although he, like so many others, did so implicitly and did not use the term "ontology" anywhere in his analysis).[32]

As a result of this aspect, manuals in the second ontological school have the potential to bring about the development of a dissonance between tactical means and strategic ends. By taking for granted answers to ontological questions about the relationship between militaries and societies and the nature of the environment in which militaries operate, manuals in the second school are susceptible to providing ill-suited guidance when faced with situations that do not match those envisaged by the ontological model they implicitly accept. For example, manuals that assume "enemy" forces will be that of another state may fail to provide adequate guidance for the conduct of operations against non-state groups. In such situations, doctrine in the second school becomes irrelevant and the success or failure of military endeavors must ultimately rely upon the abilities of individual commanders to come to an independent understanding of the broader context and act accordingly.[33]

In extreme cases the existence of tactical manuals in such situations may even be counter-productive as commanders following their guidance seek to implement tactical solutions that ultimately detract from the achievement of strategic goals. For example, it has been compellingly argued elsewhere that the dissonance between tactical "success" and strategic failure that characterized the American War in Vietnam was largely a result of the exclusively tactical nature and role of US military doctrine during that war. This problem was exacerbated because throughout that War most tactical doctrine did not align with the tactics that were required to achieve strategic success.[34]

The Operational Manual School

There can be little doubt that the American experience in Vietnam was the catalyst for the subsequent emergence within English speaking militaries of the third school of doctrinal ontology. This emergence has been labeled the US Army's "doctrinal renaissance"[35] and it has already been subjected to much intellectual scrutiny.[36] The key doctrine manual that heralded the emergence of the third ontological school is the 1982 edition of FM 100-5 *Operations*, and the process leading to the development of this manual was fundamental in establishing the new school.[37]

Following its withdrawal from Vietnam, the US Army faced significant challenges. Organizationally, these included major morale, discipline, and drug problems.[38] Operationally, the immediate needs of the Vietnam War had resulted in a decade-long disruption to the Army's planning for the defense of Western Europe. Concerns about Soviet qualitative gains during the intervening period were greatly exacerbated by the 1973 Arab-Israeli War, which dramatically demonstrated the battlefield potential of modern Soviet weapons systems.[39] Confronted with this challenge and keen to leave behind the bitter experience of the War in Vietnam (intellectually as well as in many other ways), the US Army set out to reorient itself toward winning a conventional land war in Europe.[40]

The central mechanism enabling this reorientation was doctrine. Facilitating this was the establishment of the US Army's Training and Doctrine Command (TRADOC) in 1973, initially under the command of General William E. DePuy. The 1976 edition of FM 100-5, produced under DePuy's leadership, focused on preparing the Army to "win the

19

first battle of the next war" in Europe.[41] The release of this manual prompted an unusually high amount of debate both from within and outside of the Army which led to it becoming "one of the most controversial field manuals ever published by the US Army."[42] This debate emerged primarily because the manual established a defensive operational doctrine that stood in drastic contrast to the Army's longstanding predilection for offensive operations. Because of the debate, several flaws in the tactics this manual promulgated were soon apparent.[43] Fixing these errors served as the catalyst for next round of doctrinal reform, which in turn led to the publication of the 1982 edition of FM 100-5.

Although the "AirLand Battle" concept was central to the 1982 edition of FM 100-5,[44] the manual's key ontological contribution was to assert the existence of an operational level of warfare. Stating that "operational level of war uses available military resources to attain strategic goals within a theater of war," the doctrine also determined that "military strategy employs the armed forces of a nation to secure the objectives of national policy" and that "tactics are the specific techniques smaller units use to win battles and engagements which support operational objectives."[45] In other words, this model perceives tactics as a subset of operations, which are in turn a subset of military strategy, which is itself a means of achieving national policy goals. Despite the appearance of this idea in Prussian/ German doctrine in the mid-19th century and in Russian/Soviet doctrine early in the 20th, this was the first time it had been included in the doctrine of an English speaking Western military.[46]

The reasons for the American time lag behind Prussia/Germany and Russia/Soviet are complicated and although an analysis of these reasons is not the focus of this monograph, they are nonetheless worth briefly summarizing.[47] Primarily, the time lag was caused by two factors. The first was the "American Way of War" that this monograph has already touched upon. Because this way of war stresses the exploitation of technologies to either attrit or outright annihilate the enemy, it does not require any subtlety as far as operational planning is concerned.[48] The second factor, which became important following the Second World War, was the advent of nuclear weapons. These called into question the ongoing need for operational planning, as it was initially assumed that the prospects of nuclear war would render conventional warfare redundant.[49] Despite experimentation with tactical innovations such as the "Pentomic Division," the initial impact of the debate about nuclear weapons was to stymie, until after the end of the Vietnam War, any serious attempts towards explicitly developing the operational art.[50]

When the operational level of warfare was discussed in the 1982 edition of FM 100-5, it was also the first time that a notable English-language doctrine manual had made its underlying ontology explicit. This ontology, grounded in the Clausewitzian maxim that "war is nothing but the continuation of policy with other means," established that the Army's role was subordinate to national policy.[51] It also clearly established the Army's perception of the scope of its role in relation to policy, suggesting that once policymakers had set policy goals and determined strategic objectives, the Army should be entrusted to plan and conduct operations to fulfill these objectives.[52] In making this suggestion, the manual endorsed what Eliot Cohen referred to as the "normal" theory of civil-military relations first expounded by Samuel Huntington and since enshrined as "the accepted theoretical standard" that civil-military relations should strive to attain.[53] The focus on the Soviet challenge in Europe made it clear that the Army also considered its role to be that of a "conventional" war fighting force. Furthermore, the Army was the military of a state and as such existed to undertake operations to defeat the military forces of other states. Little doubt was left as to the Army's perception of the prevailing international environment or what it understood America's key policy goals and strategic objectives to be.

The second noteworthy difference between the 1982 edition of FM 100-5 and previous doctrine was that the process used to develop and refine the new manual was a radical departure from what had previously occurred. Hitherto, doctrine had tended to be written by individuals or small teams and then circulated to a limited audience for pre-release feedback. The new process, later summarized by John Romjue, was much broader in scope:

> The development of the new doctrine was one thing, its acceptance by the Army and an influential cadre of civilian defense writers and critics was another. Fresh in memory was the debate over the 1976 version of FM 100-5 with its active defense doctrine. In 1981, TRADOC Headquarters proceeded differently from the way it had with the 1976 concept. First, [then Commander of TRADOC] General Starry took pains to include the Army at large in the development of AirLand Battle, disseminating information through briefings and wide circulation of Fort Leavenworth's draft of the new FM 100-

5 during 1981. The doctrine was well received. AirLand Battle was an offence-oriented doctrine that the Army found intellectually, as well as analytically, convincing.[54]

Together, the explicit ontology propounded within the new manual and its developers' willingness to take steps to include the Army and US defense and strategic studies communities more broadly in the doctrine development process indicate the main enduring characteristics of the third school of doctrinal ontology.

No longer was the role of doctrine limited to the dissemination of technical instructions and tactical best-practice. Instead, doctrine manuals became a mechanism for disseminating analytically sound theoretically-derived operational concepts that prompted commanders to engage with them in a much more intellectual manner than had previously been the case. Due to this intent, the third school of doctrinal ontology could be labeled the "operational manual" school. Manuals in this school have tended to be applied to provide "guidance" for operational commanders and planning staff. This doctrinal role has been accompanied by major changes in the pedagogical use of doctrine. Specifically, its usage has increased markedly in prominence within intermediate and senior level officer education courses.[55]

Over the coming years, the other branches of the US military underwent their own ontological awakening which saw their doctrine expand into the third school. For the US Marine Corps (USMC), the 1989 edition of Fleet Marine Force Manual (FMFM) 1 *Warfighting* and its accompanying publications embodied this awakening.[56] As Lieutenant Colonel H. T. Hayden later asserted, "until FMFM 1 *Warfighting*, FMFM 1-1 *Campaigning*, and FMFM 1-3 *Tactics*, not one publication taught a Marine how to think about war. Not one produced a theory of war."[57] The publication of the 1989 edition of FMFM 1 filled this void, making its ontology explicit in the process.

Like the 1982 edition of FM 100-5, the new edition of FMFM 1 explicitly recognized the existence of an operational level of warfare and in so doing, expressed the USMC's acceptance of a similar ontological outlook to that of the Army. This was not, however, the central concept featured within the manual. Instead, its key conceptual contribution was its development of maneuver warfare, which was defined as "a warfighting philosophy that seeks to shatter the enemy's cohesion through a series of rapid, violent, and unexpected actions which create a turbulent and rapidly deteriorating situation with which he cannot cope."[58] Although the Marine Corps viewed its role in relation to national policy and strategic goals in the same way as the Army, it had developed a different approach to the conduct of operations in pursuit of these goals.

The 1992 edition of Air Force Manual (AFM) 1-1 *Basic Aerospace Doctrine of the United States Air Force* was the equivalent US Air Force (USAF) publication. For the first time in USAF doctrine, this manual incorporated a discussion of the operational level of conflict. However its main conceptual contribution was the elaboration of seven "tenets of aerospace power."[59] Like the USMC, the Air Force had developed its own operational approach but nevertheless viewed its role in relation to national policy and strategy in the same way as the Army. Additionally, the manual's unique format demonstrated the expanded doctrine development process typical of the third ontological school: it contained two volumes, the first being the doctrine itself and the second featuring 25 essays that gave intellectual substance to the concepts contained in the doctrine.[60]

The US Navy (USN) also briefly flirted with the third school of doctrinal ontology during the mid-1990s following the establishment of a short-lived Naval Doctrine Command in 1993.[61] This flirtation led quickly to the publication of Naval Doctrine Publication (NDP) 1 *Naval Warfare* in 1994, which, like its equivalents in the other Services, established three levels of war.[62] Declaring that "maneuver warfare, based on the twin pillars of decisiveness and rapidity, is our preferred style of warfighting,"[63] it quite deliberately aligned the Navy's operational approach with that of the Marine Corps.[64] Thus, the ostensible ontological underpinning of the Navy's third school doctrine manual also aligned closely with the proclaimed ontological approach of the USMC. The Navy's manual, however, was notably shorter and far less detailed than its Marine Corps (or indeed Army and Air Force) equivalent. The reasons for this difference relate to both the circumstances of its development and release as well as to the service culture of the USN.

Indeed, each service's culture has played a significant if low-key role in determining the manner in which the doctrine of each has evolved.[65] In the case of the US services for example, the Army has been credited with being a "doctrine-based organization" while the Navy has generally been dismissive of doctrine development.[66] As the dissemination of the third school of doctrinal ontology illustrates, the ontological trends identified within this monograph are broadly applicable across the services. Differences in service culture are manifest as the time lag between the proliferation of each new school of doctrinal ontology within each service as well as in the terminology each has used to refer to its doctrine. A non-US example is perhaps the most strikingly illustrative: manuals in the first and second ontological schools were traditionally labeled "procedural manuals" or "fleet instructions" by Commonwealth navies and were not acknowledged as being doctrinal until the 1990s.[67]

In the US military, each service views its preferred relationship with the state in a Huntingtonian manner, seeing itself as subordinate to the state's government and acknowledging that it exists as a mechanism to implement the government's national strategy and related policies.[68] However, the means by which each service prefers to implement this strategy and policy can differ substantially.[69] This difference is partly the product of service culture, which helps to explain why there is a difference between each of the service's operational approaches described above.

Military "Thought Collectives" and Allied Doctrine Development

The third school of doctrinal ontology also spread to the militaries of key English speaking US allies. The examples of Britain, Canada, and Australia are illustrative. In Britain, the Army was the first of the three services to experiment with doctrine in the third ontological school, although the inspiration for this experimentation has been contested. on one hand, Markus Mäder, has observed that it was "in close alignment with the US Armed Forces' reorientation after the Vietnam War and their development of an **AirLand Battle** concept for the European battlefield."[70] Hew Strachan, on the other, has asserted that the intellectual inspiration for General Sir Nigel Bagnall's (Chief of the General Staff from 1985-88) decision to adopt the operational level of war was the German Army and that "the British army mirrored but was independent of comparable trends in the United States."[71] Of the two accounts, Mäder's is more closely aligned with the mainstream view and Strachan's account focuses more exclusively on Bagnall and his (considerable) individual influence.[72]

Even if Strachan is correct about the influences upon Bagnall's decision making (which is likely), developments in the US nevertheless had an impact on the intellectual debate that surrounded the emergence of the third school of doctrine in Britain. Regardless of what influenced

Bagnall personally, American developments clearly played a significant role in shaping those around him as well as in setting a tone generally for the British debate about their doctrinal direction and requirements.[73]

Following this period of debate and accompanied by changes to senior officer education programs, Britain's first third school doctrine manual, *Design for Military Operations—British Military Doctrine*, was released by the British Army in 1989.[74] The new manual discussed the levels of war and advanced the maneuverist approach as the Army's preferred operational concept.[75] Over the next half decade, "the debate over the manoeuvrist [sic] approach spread across Service boundaries and the concept was integrated into Britain's first joint doctrine in 1997."[76]

Although their militaries are substantially smaller than that of the US or even the United Kingdom (UK), Australia and Canada also expanded their doctrine into the third ontological school during the same period. In Australia, the Army was the first service to do so, addressing the operational level of war in the 1985 edition of Manual of Land Warfare (MLW) One 1.1 *Fundamentals of Land Force Operations*.[77] A decade later the Canadian Forces followed suit, releasing joint operational level doctrine in 1995.[78] The publication of these manuals was accompanied in both countries by changes to professional military education programs, although these were not as substantial as those undertaken in the militaries of their larger allies.[79]

The emergence of this school was not, however, accompanied within these allied militaries by the same broad ranging debate that constituted one of the key characteristics of its emergence within the US military. In the case of Australia, Michael Evans noted that the 1985 edition of *Fundamentals of Land Force Operations* "sought to define an Australian context for campaign planning."[80] To this end, the development of this manual was accompanied by some intellectual discussion. However, this was mostly internal to the Army and was thus limited in breadth. In the case of Canada, Howard Coombs has observed that half a dozen or so journal articles, book chapters and internal Canadian Defence College papers, and a collection of Symposium papers published in 1995, constitute the only evidence of the limited debate that occurred within the Canadian Forces.[81] Even the more extensive debate that occurred within the British Army has been described as "rather more low key" than that which occurred within the US Army.[82]

In attempting to explain this situation within the Canadian Forces,

Coombs has offered the only explanation known to this author of why this may have been the case within the militaries of any of these US allies. Applying Ludwik Fleck's concept of "thought collectives," which consist of "participants in a definable and collective structure of thought generated by an esoteric circle of authorities or experts," Coombs identified a "North American military thought collective." Regarding the emergence of operational level doctrine in Canada, he subsequently determined that:

> One must situate the paradigm shift within the context of a single group of military professionals defined by a common purpose rather than locating it in two distinct groups separated by nationality… The experts within the larger collective were the doctrine writers and then the practitioners of the United States Army…None of the hallmarks of the paradigm shift [that could be] attributed to professional discourse took place in Canada because **it had already occurred in the United States**. The Canadian military implicitly viewed itself as part of a single community of practice that extended across the continent and followed the paradigm shift that had taken place.[83]

The existence of international military "thought collectives" is an interesting notion that warrants further examination.

From the available evidence, it appears that the extent of the influence of international developments as a substitute for domestic debate is related to the size of the military in question. The larger the military, the greater the extent of the intellectual debate surrounding the emergence of the third school of doctrinal ontology. This notion aligns with Fleck's conception of the structure and pattern of communication within a thought collective. "This group [the experts] communicates knowledge within a circle of laypeople that provides feedback on these views. Knowledge passes from the inner to outer circles and back again so that this cycle is strengthened and collectivized."[84] In light of the cursory examination conducted above, it could be argued that the US Army thinkers of the late 1970s and early 1980s constituted an inner circle with Canadian and Australian thinkers situated in outer circles and their British counterparts somewhere in the middle.[85]

Yet for this to be the case, there needs to be some evidence that knowledge passes "back again" from these allies to the US military. Although there is evidence that this has occurred in a limited number of cases—for example in 2005 when the International Institute for

Strategic Studies observed that "large portions of the new US future land warfighting concept appear to have been drawn directly from the Australian Complex Warfighting doctrine"[86]—instances such as this appear to be limited to at most only a handful of cases. The rest of the time, US doctrine development has been influenced instead by domestic factors, including conceptual developments, and evaluations of America's own strategic circumstances and operational experiences.[87] As Romjue's aforementioned account of the process used to develop the 1982 edition of FM 100-5 attests, a military thought collective exists within the US wherein doctrine writers are the "experts" and the defense community contains the "laypeople" from which the experts actively seek feedback.[88] The existence of this domestic thought collective means that US doctrine writers are at liberty to ignore their smaller allies when it suits them to do so, a liberty these allies do not necessarily have themselves due to their need to remain interoperable with the US.[89]

The result is that although an international military thought collective can be identified between the US military and key English-speaking allied militaries, the flow of ideas from the inner to the outer circles is far stronger and more consistent than the return flow from the outer to inner circles. As a result of this divergence from Fleck's conception, the military thought collective also possesses the character of an "epistemic community." Described by Peter Haas as "a network of professionals with recognized expertise and competence in a particular domain and an authoritative claim to policy-relevant knowledge within that domain or issue area," epistemic communities are characterized by "a shared set of normative and principled beliefs…shared casual beliefs…shared notions of validity…[and] a common policy enterprise," rather than by the explicit transition of ideas between inner to outer circles.[90] The perception of the Canadian doctrine writers who elected to include the operational level of war in Canadian doctrine certainly viewed themselves as part of "a single group of military professionals" with their US counterparts, regardless of whether those counterparts felt likewise.[91]

Ultimately, however, developments within the US military, particularly the doctrinal embrace of the operational level of war, influenced the military intellectual communities within the allied militaries of Britain, Canada, and Australia. Despite the divergence and its implications identified above, Fleck's "thought collectives," as applied by Coombs, can be identified between the US military and these English-speaking allies. This concept will therefore be subsequently revisited from time-to-time throughout the rest of this monograph.

The Military Strategic School

By the mid-1990s the third school of doctrinal ontology had proliferated to most English speaking militaries. However, the global strategic situation was changing drastically during the same period, generating unusually high and widespread levels of strategic uncertainty for Western militaries. This uncertainty was initially generated by the fall of the Berlin Wall and the subsequent collapse of the Soviet Union. Over the next few years, this would be accompanied by Iraq's unexpected invasion of Kuwait leading to an equally unexpected US success in repelling Iraqi forces, substantial post-Cold War military budget cuts, renewed policy debate about homosexual and female integration in military and combat units, the need to integrate an array of newly emergent technologies, and finally by the onset of an awkward transition from peacekeeping to peace enforcement which involved the conduct of bloody, indecisive, or ultimately failed operations in several places, most notably Somalia and the former Yugoslavia.[92]

Together, these changes triggered a cascade of ontological (and even epistemological) questions for Western militaries. Why had the US won such an impressive victory against Iraq in 1991? How would new information technologies change the nature of warfare? What would be the American military role in what was being touted as the emerging "unipolar world"[93] and for that matter what military role would its allies (especially those in Western Europe) be expected to play given the collapse of the Soviet Union? What were the appropriate roles for Western militaries to play during peace enforcement missions? Should these missions even be considered "proper" soldiering or were they instead something less than worthy of the attention of modern military forces? Were peace enforcement missions achievable within the boundaries of existing military structures and training? Indeed, what was the appropriate structure for military forces now that the Cold War was over and the Soviet threat gone? As Western militaries sought answers to these questions, the fourth school of doctrinal ontology emerged.

This school could be labeled the "military strategic" school. This label is derived from the conceptual sub-division of the "strategic level of war" into national strategy (alternatively labeled grand strategy or national policy objectives) on one hand and military strategy on the other. In the first of these sub-divisions, governments determine overarching strategic goals that have military as well as other aspects while in the second sub-division, militaries themselves develop institutional strategies to enable them to implement the military aspects of national strategy.[94] Doctrine manuals in the military strategic school are generally referred to as "keystone" or "capstone" manuals and they usually sit at the pinnacle of formally established doctrine hierarchies.[95]

In terms of their content, doctrine manuals in the fourth school tend to be philosophical in nature, establishing fundamental principles or a core conceptual framework that is intended to describe, categorize, and justify military activities as much as guide the application of military force in pursuit of national strategic goals. Their precise content, however, varies from service to service and military to military. Michael Codner concisely summarized this variation in the case of the British armed forces:

> The Army presents a preferred style of warfare. The [Royal] Navy is cautious about prescription and offers what is essentially a conceptual framework, distilling wisdom from the corpus of work on maritime strategic theory. The Royal Air Force provides a rigorous and coherent analysis of tasks within an overall framework of principles and in so doing, makes a logical case for an independent air force.[96]

Similar variances can be observed in the case of several other armed forces including those of Canada, Australia, and New Zealand.[97]

In the US armed forces, the separation of the third and fourth schools of doctrinal ontology has been less distinct than in the militaries of these smaller allies. In the Army, USMC, and USAF, more recent editions of manuals that were formerly located unambiguously within the third school have since taken on characteristics more closely aligned with the fourth.[98]

For the Army, these characteristics first crept into the 1993 edition of FM 100-5, the second chapter of which discussed the US national strategic context and the Army's military strategic roles therein. The rest of the manual, however, continued to focus almost exclusively on the operational level of war. The subsequent edition, released in 2001 with a new reference number of FM 3-0, advocated the conduct of "full spectrum operations," a concept that linked Army operations to military strategy in a much more consistent and explicit manner throughout.[99] Another manual, FM 1 *The Army,* described in its own preface as "one of the Army's two capstone manuals" (the other being FM 3-0) has since provided an even stronger bridge between Army operations and national strategy.[100]

For the Marine Corps, the 1997 edition of Marine Corps Doctrine Publication 1 (MCDP 1—the title given to replacement manual for FMFM 1), was clearly located within the fourth school of doctrinal ontology. It provided a short introductory overview of the nature, theory, and conduct of war, leaving more specific discussion about military strategy, operations, and tactics to subsequent manuals in the series which fit within the fourth, third, and second schools respectively.[101]

The 1997 edition of *Air Force Basic Doctrine*, itself re-titled and re-numbered as Air Force Doctrine Document (AFDD) 1, included an unprecedented (in terms of USAF doctrine) discussion about the "levels of doctrine." Explicitly placing itself above operational and tactical doctrine, it subsequently confirmed its fourth school status through the inclusion of a series of lists such as "principles of war," "tenets of air and space power," and "air and space power functions."[102] While these lists were simple (perhaps even a little simplistic) in comparison to the equivalent Army and Marine Corps doctrine, they nonetheless provided a conceptually sound explanation of the USAF role in implementing US national strategy.[103]

The USN is conspicuous because it is different to the other Services. The fourth school has not emerged at all within the USN, which has instead achieved similar functions though non-doctrinal institutional strategy publications. These publications include: *...From the Sea*; *FORWARD ...From the Sea*; and *Anytime, Anywhere*.[104] Discussing these and other key US Navy strategy documents of the 1990s, Hattendorf asserted that:

> the documents assembled here, though labeled "strategic concepts," are not framed in a specific context that allows them to meet the definition of an operational strategy. In conceptual terms, they are closer to doctrine than to strategy. Actually, they lie between doctrine and strategy as strictly defined.[105]

As Hattendorf's definition of doctrine is reminiscent of the third ontological school discussed above (it "addresses how one generally expects, or even prefers, to **operate** to carry out the broad missions that are likely to appear in future scenarios"), his assertion about these documents reveals their similarity to doctrine in the fourth school.[106]

Finally, the 1990s saw the emergence of "joint" doctrine which involved the proliferation of manuals applicable to all of the services. In the US, this doctrine emerged following the 1986 passage of the Goldwater-Nichols Department of Defense Reorganization Act, which was designed to balance single service interests with joint operational and organizational imperatives.[107] The Act stimulated a great momentum in the US military towards jointness and a joint capstone doctrine manual, Joint Publication (JP) 1 *Joint Warfare of the US Armed Forces*, was released in November 1991.[108]

Other English speaking militaries followed suit during the 1990s or early 2000s although they differed from the US in one major way, the publication of their own joint doctrine tended to be internally driven by their armed forces. Where US joint doctrine had been produced because of a legislative catalyst (the Goldwater-Nichols Reorganization Act), the move towards jointness on the part of its English speaking allies was the product of armed forces reacting to post-Cold War budget cuts. These cuts initially brought about the amalgamation of functions previously duplicated by each service (such as aspects of logistics) with subsequent reforms eventually leading to the establishment of permanent joint command structures.[109] Importantly, newly established joint structures usually had an operational or strategic focus, leaving tactical activities to each of the services. The result of this focus was that new joint doctrine manuals produced to detail the function of these structures tended to fit within the third or fourth schools, with occasional manuals in the second and virtually none in the first.[110]

One of the key distinctive features of doctrine manuals in the fourth school is their intended audience. The intended audience of the fourth school is much broader while doctrine in the first three schools is intended either exclusively or primarily for an internal service audience. In addition to the service audience it includes members of other services, other government departments, the members of legislative and executive branches of government, allied militaries, and the general public. The 2005 edition of the US Army's FM 1, for example, states upfront that its intended audience "includes the Executive Branch, Congress, Office of the Secretary of Defense, Joint Staff, combatant commanders, other Services, officers, non-commissioned officers, and enlisted Soldiers of all Army components, and Army civilians."[111]

Furthermore, this school of doctrine is intended to perform a different function for each of these audiences. In addition to providing military strategic level guidance for its internal audience (a similar function to that of doctrine in the third school), it also constitutes an open and accessible declaration of institutional strategy, a platform for supporting service lobbying, and a public relations tool.[112] Part of these roles has also been to explain how a service contributes to implementing national strategy and strategic policy. Hence in the US case, documents such as

31

the National Security Strategy, National Military Strategy, and Defense Planning Guidance are taken into account during the development of these manuals.[113] Yet surprisingly little analysis of the significance and impact of these additional aspects has been undertaken and the scope of fourth school doctrine manuals is often overlooked. Perhaps this is because declarations such as those appearing in FM 1 are the exception, not the rule. Usually, the external audience of fourth school doctrine manuals tends not to be explicitly mentioned within them.[114]

Although doctrine in the fourth school has maintained some key ontological features of the third school, it has in other respects diverged greatly. Separating it from the third school is the greatly expanded, and for that matter not-so-well defined, scope of its focus. That it could be labeled "military strategic" rather than "operational" is indicative of this. Closely related to this difference in scope is the uncertainty confronting militaries during the 1990s. This starkly contrasts with the final decade of the Cold War when the third school of doctrinal ontology emerged, during which period Western militaries faced a single specific threat that was clearly definable in nature and origin. Accompanying this was an ontological clarity that was suddenly missing following the collapse of the Soviet Union.

In the face of the uncertainty that followed, doctrine became at once "the military's instrument for analyzing past experience, guiding current operations, and exploring future challenges" or what could be labeled an "instrument for analysis."[115] In other words, as militaries struggled to determine the nature and extent of their post-Cold War roles, doctrine in the fourth school emerged as a mechanism enabling them to undertake an institutional exploration of the key ontological challenges they were confronting.

In a few significant ways, doctrine in the fourth school is similar to that in the third. It plays a vital role in establishing the military's perception of its role in relation to society, the state, and government policy for example. It also constitutes a mechanism for disseminating theoretically derived concepts that prompt intellectual engagement, however evidence of the ontological uncertainty of the period abounds in the plethora of new concepts that have been included in the doctrine manuals that together constitute the fourth school. These concepts have notably included the Revolution in Military Affairs (RMA), effects based operations (EBO), network centric warfare (NCW), military operations other than war (MOOTW), stability and support operations (SASO), and rapid decisive operations (RDO) to name but a few.[116]

In addition, maneuver warfare, conceptually expanded and rebadged as "the maneuverist approach," has been particularly prevalent within military strategic doctrine, possibly owing to the flexibility with which it can be applied.[117]

Finally, as the concepts contained in fourth school doctrine manuals have been derived from a mixture of military and external sources, their development represents yet another difference from manuals in the other schools. While first and second school manuals were usually developed by individuals or small groups of officers, usually writing within staff colleges or general staffs,[118] third school manuals usually contain concepts of internal military origin that may have been subsequently refined in consultation with outsiders.[119] The fourth school, however, draws on concepts developed both internally to militaries and externally by defense academics, commentators, and other members of the defense community. This is likely another product of the uncertainty of the era in which fourth school doctrine emerged. As militaries attempted to make sense of the changed environment and their roles within it, they became more willing to consider ideas from a broader variety of sources.

Notes

1.   John Childs, "The Military Revolution I: The Transition to Modern Warfare," in Charles Townshend, ed., *The Oxford Illustrated History of Modern War,* Oxford: Oxford University Press, 1997, pp. 32-3. This is the traceable, unbroken lineage of contemporary written doctrine. Although some have argued that certain Roman treatises constituted doctrine in a similar form to that of the modern era, the accuracy of this argument depends on the definition of the term "doctrine" that is applied. For example, Richard M. van Nort, *The Battle of Adrianople and the Military Doctrine of Vegitius,* The City University of New York: Unpublished PhD Dissertation, 2007, asserts that Roman Legions regularly applied doctrine as a matter of routine. Although he appears to equate the term "doctrine" to both military theory and tactics, van Nort does not explicitly define the term itself, hence leaving the nature of its relationship to modern doctrine open to debate. Regarding *Wapenhandlingen van Roers, Musqetten ende Spiessen,* Feld has observed that it was "obviously influenced by the numerous fencing books printed throughout Europe after about 1530." Importantly, it differed from these earlier texts in two substantial ways. First, its intended audience was militaries rather than the general public, and second, the level of procedural detail with which it treated its subject meant that it constituted "an integrated instructional device, perhaps the first ever printed." M. D. Feld, "Middle-Class Society and the Rise of Military Professionalism: The Dutch Army 1589-1609," *Armed Forces and Society*, Vol. 1, No. 4, August 1975, pp. 423-4.

2.   Childs, "The Military Revolution I," pp. 19-34; Jeremy Black, "The Military Revolution II: Eighteenth-Century War," in Townshend, ed., *The Oxford Illustrated History of Modern War,* pp. 35-47.

3.   Bruce D. Porter, *War and the Rise of the State: The Military Foundations of Modern Politics,* New York, NY: The Free Press, 1994, pp. 64-7, 110-3.

4.   For further details about the significance and effect of these treaties, see: Kalevi J. Holsti, *Peace and War: Armed Conflicts and International Order 1648-1989*, Cambridge Studies in International Relations No. 14, Cambridge: Cambridge University Press, 1991, pp. 25-42. The relationship between doctrine and the emergence and evolution of the modern, state-centric international system is further discussed in the third chapter.

5.   Childs, "The Military Revolution I," p. 33.

6.   In making this observation it must be remembered that during this period "modern" militaries had not yet been fully institutionalized, even within the most "advanced" European states. For this reason, they cannot be expected by this era to have developed an institutional discourse. Charles Tilly, *Coercion, Capital, and European States, AD 990-1992,* Oxford: Blackwell, 1992, pp. 67-95.

7. Brian McAllister Linn, *The Echo of Battle: The Army's Way of War*, Cambridge, MA: Harvard University Press, 2007, pp. 200-1.

8. Another example of this "macro" effect is the influence of marksmanship training on U.S. Army culture and weapons acquisition decisions. See: Thomas L. McNaugher, *Marksmanship, McNamara and the M16 Rifle: Organizations, Analysis and Weapons Acquisition*, RAND Paper No. P-6306, Santa Monica, CA: RAND Corporation, March 1979.

9. For example, see: John S. Clay, "The Fifth Service Looks at Doctrine," *Joint Force Quarterly*, No. 14, Winter 1996-7, pp. 29-33.

10. Gary Sheffield, "Doctrine and Command in the British Army: An Historical Overview," in Directorate General Development and Doctrine, *Army Doctrine Publication: Land Operations,* United Kingdom: British Army, May 2005, p. 165.

11. James J. Tritten, "Developing Naval Doctrine ...*From the Sea,*" *Joint Force Quarterly*, No. 9, Autumn 1995, p. 111; Michael Codner, "British Maritime Doctrine and National Military Strategy," in Centre for Defence Studies, Kings College London, *Brassey's Defence Yearbook 1996,* London: Brassey's, 1996, pp. 88-104; Aaron P. Jackson, *Doctrine Development in Five Commonwealth Navies: A Comparative Perspective*, Papers in Australian Maritime Affairs No. 33, Canberra: Sea Power Centre—Australia, 2010, p. 1; Robert Futrell, *Ideas, Concepts, Doctrine: Volume I: Basic Thinking in the United States Air Force 1907-1960,* Maxwell Air force Base: Air University Press, 1989, p. xi; Aaron P. Jackson, "The Emergence of a "Doctrinal Culture" within the Canadian Air Force: Where it Came From, Where it's at and Where to From Here? Part One: Doctrine and Canadian Air Force Culture Prior to the End of the Cold War," *Canadian Air Force Journal*, Vol. 2, No. 3, Summer 2009, pp. 38-46.

12. Examples of these alternative perspectives include: P. Richard Moller, "The Dangers of Doctrine," in *Maritime Security Working Paper No. 5,* Halifax: Dalhousie University, December 1996, pp. 57-71; Milan Vego, *Joint Operational Warfare: Theory and Practice,* Newport RI: U.S. Naval War College, 2007, pp. XII.4-XII.6.

13. Holsti, *Peace and War*, pp. 46-63; Black, "The Military Revolution II," pp. 35-47.

14. Holsti, *Peace and War*, p. 63.

15. Black, "The Military Revolution II," p. 45.

16. Hal Klepak, "Some Reflections on Generalship Through the Ages," in Bernd Horn & Stephen J. Harris, eds., *Generalship and the Art of the Admiral: Perspectives on Canadian Senior Military Leadership,* St. Catherines, ON: Vanwell Publishing, 2001, pp. 24-5; Lynn, *Battle*, pp. 137-9.

17. For a detailed discussion about the nature and extent of the works of these and other key military thinkers of the late 18th century, see: Azar Gat, *A History of Military Thought: From the Enlightenment to the Cold War*, Oxford: Oxford University Press, 2001, Bk I, pp. 27-55.

18. Walter E. Kretchik, *U.S. Army Doctrine: From the American Revolution to the War on Terror,* Lawrence, KS: University Press of Kansas, 2011, pp. 16-24.

19. Paul Johnston, "Doctrine is Not Enough: The Effect of Doctrine on the Behavior of Armies," *Parameters*, Vol. XXX, No. 3, Autumn 2000, pp. 31-2.

20. John A. Lynn, *Battle: A History of Combat and Culture,* Cambridge, MA: Westview, 2003, pp. 179-200.

21. Bernard Brodie, *War and Politics,* New York: MacMillan Publishing Co., 1973, pp. 252-8.

22. Michael Mann, *The Sources of Social Power: Volume II: The Rise of Classes and Nation-States, 1760-1914,* Cambridge, UK: Cambridge University Press, 1993, pp. 419-36.

23. John Gooch, "Introduction: Military Doctrine in Military History," in John Gooch, ed., *The Origins of Contemporary Doctrine*, Occasional Paper No. 30, Camberly: Strategic and Combat Studies Institute, September 1997, p. 5; Gat, *A History of Military Thought*, Bk II, pp. 269-72, 285. For a discussion of the impact of the Enlightenment on the development of military theory, see Gat, Bk I, part 1.

24. On the works of Jomini and their influence, see: John Shy, "Jomini," in Peter Paret, ed., *Makers of Modern Strategy: From Machiavelli to the Nuclear Age,* Princeton, NJ: Princeton University Press, 1986, pp. 143-85; Gat, *A History of Military Thought*, Bk I, pp. 108-137.

25. John L. Romjue, "The Evolution of American Army Doctrine," in Gooch, ed., *The Origins of Contemporary Doctrine*, pp. 52-3.

26. Romjue, "The Evolution of American Army Doctrine," p. 53.

27. Christopher R. Gabel, "Preface," in U.S. Army, FM 100-5 *Field Service Regulations: Operations* [first issued 1941]. Fort Leavenworth: U.S. Army Command and General Staff College Press, 1992.

28. U.S. Army, FM 100-5, 1941, p. ii.

29. The idea that universal principles of war existed and could be uncovered and applied to guide all military operations regardless of the unique circumstances of individual wars, campaigns and battles, first gained prominence during the late Renaissance. This idea was subsequently shaped, and greatly popularized, by the prevailing intellectual paradigms of the Enlightenment, and the notion has remained (rightly or wrongly) within the discourse of military theory ever since. Gat, *A History of Military Thought*, Bk I, part 1. See also: John A. Alger, *The Quest for Victory: The History of the*

Principles of War, Contributions in Military History No. 30, Westport, CT: Greenwood Press, 1982, which traces the routes of the principles of war to Sun Tzu, but nevertheless observes that their popularization within the West began during the 18th century.

30. Echevarria's insight is itself an indication of the implicit ontological assumptions made within tactical doctrine. In this case the assumption is that war is the province of states, while battle is the province of armies. Antulio J. Echevarria II, *Toward an American Way of War*, Carlisle: U.S. Army War College Strategic Studies Institute, March 2004.

31. The idea of a distinctive "American Way of War" was first explicitly elaborated in: Russell F. Weigley, *The American Way of War: A History of U.S. Military Strategy and Policy*, Bloomington, IN: Indiana University Press, 1973; a succinct summary of the causes and origins of this approach are also given in: John Ellis, *The Social History of the Machine Gun*, London: Pimlico, 1976, pp. 21-25 (albeit that Ellis does not use the same label as Weigley).

32. Ellis, *The Social History of the Machine Gun*, pp. 111-145.

33. There have of course been many second school doctrine manuals that address how to combat non-state groups. The assertion here is not that there has not been, but rather that different approaches are needed to meet different challenges. This doctrine only becomes irrelevant if the manuals available (or consulted) do not contain the appropriate approach for addressing the challenge at hand. On second school doctrine written about how to combat non-state groups, see: Max Boot, *The Savage Wars of Peace: Small Wars and the Rise of American Power*, New York: Basic Books, 2002, pp. 281-5; Tim Moreman, "'The Greatest Training Ground in the World': The Army in India and the North-West Frontier, 1901-1947," in Daniel P. Marston & Chandar S. Sundaram, *A Military History of India and South Asia: From the East India Company to the Nuclear Era*, Bloomington, IN: Indiana University Press, 2008, pp. 53-73.

34. Andrew F. Krepinevich, *The Army and Vietnam*, Baltimore, MD: The John Hopkins University Press, 1986.

35. Romjue, "The Evolution of American Army Doctrine," p. 70. The term "revolution in Army thinking" has also been used in reference to the same events. Richard Lock-Pullan, *U.S. Intervention Policy and Army Innovation: From Vietnam to Iraq*, New York, NY: Routledge, 2006, p. 77.

36. For example, see: Roger J. Spiller, "In the Shadow of the Dragon: Doctrine and the U.S. Army after Vietnam," in Jeffrey Grey & Peter Dennis, eds., *From Past to Future: The Australian Experience of Land/Air Operations*, Canberra: Australian Defence Force Academy, 1995, pp. 6-46; Richard Lock-Pullan, "How to Rethink War: Conceptual Innovation and AirLand Battle Doctrine," *Journal of Strategic Studies*, Vol. 28, No. 4, August 2005, pp. 679-702; Robert T. Davis II, *The Challenge of Adaptation: The U.S. Army in the Aftermath of Conflict, 1953-2000*, Fort Leavenworth KS: Combat Studies Institute Press, March 2008, pp. 45-80.

37.   Headquarters, Department of the Army, FM 100-5 *Operations,* Washington DC: U.S. Government Printing Office, August 20, 1982.

38.   Spiller, "In the Shadow of the Dragon," pp. 15-6.

39.   In Spiller's words, "the October War had the effect of organizing knowledge in the absence of operational theory. What had been until now a collection of undifferentiated suppositions and disparate intentions was given substance and an organized framework from which specific reforms could be undertaken." Spiller, p. 27.

40.   Conrad Crane presents a comprehensive analysis of the U.S. Army's intellectual desire to leave Vietnam behind, concluding that "many of the reformers who developed AirLand Battle doctrine and the force to apply it were motivated by a sense of indignation and embarrassment about losing in Southeast Asia. Out of that defeat the Army developed a new doctrine, force structure, and attitude designed to win an 'anti-Vietnam,' high-intensity conflict with the Soviets in Europe." Perhaps more revealing is a quote attributed to General Starry, one of the primary architects of the Army's post-Vietnam doctrinal reform: "After getting out of Vietnam, the Army looked around and realized it should not try to fight that kind of war again." Conrad C. Crane, *Avoiding Vietnam: The U.S. Army's Response to Defeat in Southeast Asia,* Carlisle, PA: U.S. Army Strategic Studies Institute, September 2002, pp. 16-17.

41.   Headquarters, Department of the Army, FM 100-5 *Operations,* Washington DC: U.S. Government Printing Office, July 1, 1976, p. 1.1.

42.   Robert A. Doughty, *The Evolution of U.S. Army Tactical Doctrine, 1946-76,* Leavenworth Papers No. 1, Fort Leavenworth KS: Combat Studies Institute, August 1979, p. 43.

43.   For the purposes of this monograph, details of the content of this manual are less important than the process and debate surrounding its development. Readers interested in more details about the content of this manual and the criticisms it drew are encouraged to consult: Doughty, pp. 40-6.

44.   For a concise overview of the "AirLand Battle" concept, see: John L. Romjue, "The Evolution of the AirLand Battle Concept," *Air University Review,* May-June 1984. Available from *www.airpower.maxwell.af.mil/airchronicles/aureview/1984/may-jun/romjue.html,* accessed on November 30, 2009.

45.   Headquarters, Department of the Army, FM 100-5 *Operations,* 1982, p. 2.3.

46.   The implications of this for the Prussian/German and Russian/Soviet militaries are that in these militaries the second and third schools of doctrinal ontology appeared in a much closer succession than they did in the English speaking militaries that are the subject of discussion herein. Because of the limits of this study (it's focus on English speaking militaries) the implications of this difference are not discussed here. On the reasons for the U.S. lag behind Germany and Russia, see: Vego, *Joint Operational Warfare,* pp. I.15-I.34,

XII.4; James J. Schneider, *The Structure of Strategic Revolution: Total War and the Roots of the Soviet Warfare State,* Novato CA: Presidio Press, 1994, esp. chap. 5; Shimon Naveh, *In Pursuit of Military Excellence: The Evolution of Operational Theory,* London: Frank Cass, 1997; Dennis E. Showalter, "Prussian-German Operational Art, 1740-1943" and Jacob W. Kipp, "The Tsarist and Soviet Operational Art, 1853-1991," both in John Andreas Olsen & Martin van Creveld, *The Evolution of Operational Art: From Napoleon to the Present,* Oxford: Oxford University Press, 2011, pp. 35-95.

47. For a more detailed account see: Antulio J. Echevarria II, "American Operational Art, 1917-2008," in Olsen & van Creveld, *The Evolution of Operational Art,* pp. 137-165.

48. Weigley, *The American Way of War,* p 475.

49. Michael Carver, "Conventional Warfare in the Nuclear Age," in Paret, ed., *Makers of Modern Strategy,* pp. 779-814.

50. A. J. Bacevich, *The Pentomic Era: The U.S. Army between Korea and Vietnam,* Washington, DC: National Defense University Press, 1986, esp. pp. 103-119; Echevarria, "American Operational Art," pp. 154-5.

51. Carl von Clausewitz, *On War,* edited and translated by Michael Howard and Peter Paret, Princeton NJ: Princeton University Press, 1989, p. 69.

52. This aligns with the implicit assumptions underlying several U.S. Army manuals that fall within in the tactical manual school. The key difference is that discussion within the 1982 edition of FM 100-5 was more detailed and the implications of this ontological model were finally made explicit.

53. Eliot A. Cohen, *Supreme Command: Soldiers, Statesmen and Leadership in Wartime,* New York: The Free Press, 2002, p. 226; see also Samuel P. Huntington, *The Soldier and the State: The Theory and Politics of Civil-Military Relations,* Cambridge, MA: Harvard University Press, 1959; Edward M. Coffman, "The Long Shadow of *The Soldier and the State,*" *Journal of Military History,* Vol. 55, No. 1, January 1991, pp. 69-82. Of note, subscription to the "normal" school of civil-military relations has not been limited to FM 100-5: Cohen explicitly states that FM 1 *The Army,* which fits within the fourth school of doctrinal ontology, is "largely Huntington in tone" and "a particularly interesting document". Cohen, p. 273 (n. 4).

54. Romjue, "The Evolution of the AirLand Battle Concept".

55. Linn, *The Echo of Battle,* pp. 211-212, describes the U.S. Army's experience. For examples of this effect in two allied militaries, see: Hew Strachan, "Operational Art in Britain, 1909-2009," in Olsen & van Creveld, *The Evolution of Operational Art,* p. 120; Howard G. Coombs, "In the Wake of a Paradigm Shift: The Canadian Forces College and the Operational Level of War (1987-1995)," *Canadian Military Journal,* Vol. 10 No. 2, 2010, pp. 19-27.

56. Headquarters, U.S. Marine Corps, FMFM 1 *Warfighting,* Washington, DC: U.S. Government Printing Office, March 6, 1989.

57. H. T. Hayden, "Introduction: The History and Execution of Marine Corps Doctrine," in H. T. Hayden, ed., *Warfighting: Maneuver Warfare in the U.S. Marine Corps*, London: Greenhill Books, 1995, p. 19.

58. Headquarters, U.S. Marine Corps, FMFM 1, 1989, p. 59.

59. Headquarters, U.S. Air Force, Air Force Manual (AFM) 1-1 (Volume

1), *Basic Aerospace Doctrine of the United States Air Force,* Washington, DC: U.S. Government Printing Office, March 1992, pp. 7-8.

60. Headquarters, U.S. Air Force, AFM 1-1 (Volume 2), *Basic Aerospace Doctrine of the United States Air Force,* Washington, DC: U.S. Government Printing Office, March 1992. The authorship of these essays was not disclosed.

61. Naval Doctrine Command was subsequently disestablished in 1998, at which time most of its functions were transferred to the newly established Navy Warfare Development Command. John B. Hattendorf, "Introduction," in John B. Hattendorf, ed., *U.S. Naval Strategy in the 1990s: Selected Documents,* Newport Paper No. 27, Newport, RI: Naval War College Press, 2006, p. 15.

62. Headquarters, Department of the Navy, Navy Doctrine Publication (NDP) 1 *Naval Warfare,* Washington, DC: U.S. Government Printing Office, March 28, 1994, pp. 16-7.

63. Headquarters, Department of the Navy, NDP 1 *Naval Warfare*, p. 35.

64. Hattendorf, "Introduction," p. 15.

65. There are very few available sources that address service culture in depth. Key among the sources available are: Carl H. Builder *The Masks of War: American Military Styles in Strategy and Analysis,* Baltimore MD: John Hopkins University Press, 1989; Allan D. English, *Understanding Military Culture: A Canadian Perspective,* Montreal, QC: McGill-Queens University Press, 2004.

66. U.S. Army Combined Arms Centre, "Doctrine Development", available from *http://usacac.army.mil/CAC/doctrine.asp*, accessed on August 8, 2010; Tritten, "Developing Naval Doctrine *...From the Sea,*" p. 111.

67. Jackson, *Doctrine Development in Five Commonwealth Navies*, p. 1.

68. Huntington, *The Soldier and the State*, part 1; see also Cohen, *Supreme Command*, pp. 225-248.

69. Builder, *The Masks of War*, esp. chap. 6-8.

70. Original emphasis. Markus Mäder, *In Pursuit of Conceptual Excellence: The Evolution of British Military-Strategic Doctrine in the Post-Cold War Era, 1989-2002*, Studies in Contemporary History and Security Policy No. 13, Bern: Peter Lang, 2004, p. 78.

71. Strachan, "Operational Art in Britain," pp. 119-121, quote p. 119.

72. Strachan's account is also brief, although he does note that "Bagnall's contribution is still in need of a full study." Strachan, "Operational Art in Britain," p. 135 (n. 83).

73. Mäder, *In Pursuit of Conceptual Excellence*, pp. 90-2.

74. Mäder, *In Pursuit of Conceptual Excellence*, pp. 78-103; Sheffield, "Doctrine and Command in the British Army," pp. 177-178.

75. Prepared under the Direction of the Chief of the General Staff, *Design for Military Operations—British Military Doctrine,* London: Her Majesty's Stationary Office, 1989.

76. Mäder, *In Pursuit of Conceptual Excellence*, p. 98.

77. Evans, *Forward from the Past*, p. 28.

78. Canadian Forces, *Joint and Combined Operations,* Ottawa: Canadian National Defence Headquarters, 1995.

79. Coombs, "In the Wake of a Paradigm Shift", pp. 19-27; David Cox & Andrew O'Neil, "Professional Military Education in Australia: Has it All Gone Terribly Right?" *Australian Defence Force Journal*, No. 171, 2006, pp. 59-60.

80. Evans, *Forward from the Past*, p. 28.

81. Coombs, "In the Wake of a Paradigm Shift," p. 25.

82. Sheffield, "Doctrine and Command in the British Army," p. 177.

83. Original emphasis. Coombs, "In the Wake of a Paradigm Shift," p. 25.

84. Coombs, "In the Wake of a Paradigm Shift," p. 25.

85. An interesting aside is that New Zealand not only fits within this construct, but occupies a position where one would logically expect to find it given the small size of its military relative to the other English-speaking militaries examined. Each of its Services briefly engaged in the production of third and fourth school doctrine during the early and mid-1990s, prior to deferring to foreign, usually Australian, doctrine, in lieu of undertaking further internal doctrine development in these schools. Since the early-2000s the New Zealand Defence Force has produced comprehensive joint doctrine manuals that fit within both of these schools, with the content of these manuals being strongly influenced by conceptual developments featured in allied doctrine, again primarily that of Australia. Thus, relative to the U.S., New Zealand appears to be situated in a more outer circle than either Canada or Australia, although another thought community also appears extant wherein Australian doctrine writers occupy an inner circle and New Zealand doctrine writers an outer circle. For further details about doctrine development in New Zealand, see: Aaron P. Jackson, "Getting it Right? Military-Strategic Level Doctrine Development in New Zealand," *New Zealand Journal of Defence Studies*, Vol. 3, August 2008, pp. 11-17.

86. International Institute for Strategic Studies, "Complex Irregular Warfare: The Face of Contemporary Conflict," *The Military Balance*, Vol. 105, No. 1, 2005, p. 419.

87. These developments are discussed in greater detail in subsequent chapters.

88. Romjue, "The Evolution of the AirLand Battle Concept".

89. Even though the U.S. military stresses the need for interoperability and constantly takes measures to enhance it, interoperability is nevertheless a more pressing concern for its smaller allies. The reasons for this are summarized by Middlemiss and Stairs: "It should be clear that, in any military alliance, interoperability is primarily an issue for the lesser powers. This is because it is the lesser powers that must deal with the military equivalent of "keeping up with the Joneses." Nowhere has this been more starkly revealed than in NATO, where all the members, save in some degree the United Kingdom and France, have found it a perennially daunting challenge to maintain military forces that can operate effectively with the vastly superior military establishment of the United States.", Danford W. Middlemiss & Denis Stairs, *The Canadian Forces and the Doctrine of Interoperability: The Issues*, Policy Matters Occasional Paper Series, Vol. 3, No. 7, Montreal, QC: Institute for Research on Public Policy, June 2002, p. 14.

90. Peter Haas, "Introduction: Epistemic Communities and International Policy Coordination," *International Organization*, Vol. 46, No. 1, Winter 1992, p. 3.

91. Coombs, "In the Wake of a Paradigm Shift," p. 25.

92. For a comparative analysis of Western military responses to these challenges during the 1990s, see: Charles C. Moskos, John Allan Williams & David R. Segal, eds., *The Postmodern Military: Armed Forces after the Cold War,* New York, NY: Oxford University Press, 2000.

93. For a prominent example of this debate, see: Charles Krauthammer, "The Unipolar Moment," *Foreign Affairs*, Vol. 70, No. 1, Winter 1990-1, pp. 23-33.

94. This division has been promulgated within some capstone doctrine manuals. See, for example: British Armed Forces, Joint Warfare Publication (JWP) 0-01 *British Defence Doctrine*, 1st ed., London: Her Britannic Majesty's Stationary Office, 1997, pp. 1.8-1.9; Australian Defence Force, Australian Defence Doctrine Publication-Doctrine (ADDP-D) *Foundations of Australian Military Doctrine*, 2nd ed., Canberra: Defence Publishing Service, July 2005, para. 1.7.

95. Doctrine hierarchies have long contained designated keystone or capstone manuals. Prior to the emergence of the fourth school of doctrinal ontology, these manuals were often accompanied by several other manuals in the hierarchy that fit within the same ontological school. The important difference between these and manuals in the fourth school is that fourth school manuals are generally the only manual of their school within a hierarchy. Below them, it is common to find the remainder of the hierarchy consists of several operational, tactical and technical manuals.

96. Michael Codner, "Purple Prose and Purple Passion: The Joint Defence Centre," *RU.S.I Journal*, Vol. 144, No. 1, February/March 1999, p. 38.

97. In a study of military strategic doctrine in these three countries, this author found several similarities between each army, navy and air force, but few similarities between the three services of each country. The key reason for this was service culture, which caused army doctrine to have a "downwards" focus (providing guidance for operational conduct was the key concern), navy doctrine to have an "upwards" focus (justifying funding for acquisitions to government was the key concern) and air force doctrine had an "inwards" focus (educating airmen about the significance of air power was the key concern). Interestingly, joint doctrine exhibited elements of all three of these foci as well as a fourth, "outwards" focus, to which end it was employed as a device for explaining military strategy to the general public. Aaron P. Jackson, *Doctrine, Strategy and Military Culture: Military-Strategic Doctrine Development in Australia, Canada and New Zealand, 1987-2007,* Trenton, ON: Canadian Forces Aerospace Warfare Centre, 2013.

98. A holistic study of U.S. military strategic doctrine development and its impact is notably absent from the existing literature. Although some, such as Chapman, provide a starting point, their work is nonetheless limited. Chapman, for example, focuses on doctrine development since World War Two, providing a general overview rather than examining military strategic doctrine development specifically. As his main objective is to identify sources available for further research, his analysis is understandably limited. In contrast, the development and significance of military strategic doctrine in Britain, Australia, Canada and New Zealand has been the subject of comprehensive analysis. See: Mäder, *In Pursuit of Conceptual Excellence*; Jackson, *Doctrine, Strategy and Military Culture*; Bert Chapman, *Military Doctrine: A Reference Handbook,* Santa Barbara, CA: Praeger Security International, 2009, pp. 6-41.

99. Headquarters, Department of the Army, FM 100-5 *Operations,* Washington DC: U.S. Government Printing Office, June 14, 1993; Headquarters, Department of the Army, FM 3-0 *Operations,* Washington DC: U.S. Government Printing Office, June 14, 2001.

100. This manual is not as well known as FM 3-0 and its impact is quite limited by comparison. Headquarters, Department of the Army, FM 1 *The Army,* Washington DC: U.S. Government Printing Office, June 14, 2001; since superseded by: Headquarters, Department of the Army, FM 1 *The Army,* Washington DC: U.S. Government Printing Office, June 2005.

101. Headquarters, U.S. Marine Corps, Marine Corps Doctrine Publication (MCDP) 1 *Warfighting,* Washington DC: U.S. Government Printing Office, June 20, 1997; Headquarters, U.S. Marine Corps, MCDP 1-1 *Strategy,* Washington DC: U.S. Government Printing Office, November 12, 1997; Headquarters, U.S. Marine Corps, MCDP 1-2 *Campaigning,* Washington DC: U.S. Government Printing Office, August 1, 1997; Headquarters, U.S. Marine Corps, MCDP 1-3 *Tactics,* Washington DC: U.S. Government Printing Office, July 30, 1997.

102.U.S. Air Force, Air Force Doctrine Document (AFDD) 1 *Air Force Basic Doctrine,* Maxwell Air Force Base: Headquarters Air Force Doctrine Centre, September 1997.

103.These lists were simple in the sense that they were descriptive and exhibited a straightforward, "check-list" type of appearance. This is in contrast with the equivalent Army and U.S.MC doctrine manuals, which each presented a few major thematic concepts that were explicitly linked to national strategy.

104. These and five other U.S.N strategy documents first published during the 1990s are reproduced in: Hattendorf, ed., *U.S. Naval Strategy in the 1990s.* A brief overview of the circumstances surrounding the development and release of each document is also given in this source.

105.Hattendorf, "Introduction," p. 2.

106.Added emphasis. Hattendorf, p. 3.

107.For a detailed review of the Goldwater-Nichols Reorganization Act, see: James R. Locher, "Has it Worked? The Goldwater-Nichols Reorganization Act," *Naval War College Review*, Vol. LIV, No. 4, Autumn 2001, pp. 95-115.

108.Joint Chiefs of Staff, U.S. Department of Defense, JP 1 *Joint Warfare of the U.S. Armed Forces,* Washington, DC: U.S. Government Printing Office, November 11, 1991.

109.On joint doctrine development in the UK, Australia, Canada and New Zealand, see: Mäder, *In Pursuit of Conceptual Excellence*, pp. 229-258; Jackson, *Doctrine, Strategy and Military Culture*, chap. 7.

110. Mäder, *In Pursuit of Conceptual Excellence*, pp. 297-311; Jackson, *Doctrine, Strategy and Military Culture*, chap. 7.

111. Headquarters, Department of the Army, FM 1, 2005, p. iii.

112. Kretchik, *U.S. Army Doctrine*, pp. 278-286.

113. Chiefs of Staff, U.S. Department of Defense, JP 1 *Joint Warfare of the Armed Forces of the United States*, Washington, DC: U.S. Government Printing Office, November 14, 2000, esp. foreword & chaps. 1 & 4; U.S. Navy, "NDP-1 Naval Warfare," "The Navy Operational Concept," "Anytime, Anywhere: A Navy for the 21st Century," and "Navy Strategic Planning Guidance with Long Range Guidance," all reproduced in Hattendorf, ed., *U.S. Naval Strategy in the 1990s*, pp. 136, 159-61, 171-2, 173, 177, 210, 219-20; Headquarters, Department of the Army, FM 1, June 14, 2001, pp. iv, 17-18; U.S. Air Force, AFDD 1, September 1997, pp. 5-6.

114. This is also the case regarding allied joint doctrine. See: Mäder, *In Pursuit of Conceptual Excellence*, pp. 297-311; Jackson, *Doctrine, Strategy and Military Culture*, conclusion.

115. Mäder, *In Pursuit of Conceptual Excellence*, p. 22.

116. For details of the evolution of each of these concepts, see respectively: David Jablonsky, "U.S. Military Doctrine and the Revolution in Military Affairs," *Parameters*, Vol. 24, No. 3, Autumn 1994, pp. 18-36; Paul T. Mitchell, "EBO: Thinking Effects and Effective Thinking," *Pointer*, Vol. 33, No. 1, 2007, pp. 50-58; Arthur K. Cebrowski & John J. Garstka, "Network-Centric Warfare: Its Origin and Future," *Proceedings*, Vol. 124, No. 1, January 1998, pp. 28-35; Keith E. Bonn & Anthony E. Baker, *Guide to Military Operations Other Than War: Tactics, Techniques, and Procedures for Stability and Support Operations: Domestic and International*, Mechanicsburg PA: Stackpole Books, 2000, pp. 1-20; Jennifer Morrison Taw, "Stability and Support Operations: History and Debates," *Studies in Conflict and Terrorism*, Vol. 33, No. 5, 2010, pp. 387-407; Antulio J. Echevarria II, *Rapid Decisive Operations: An Assumptions-Based Critique*, Carlisle, PA: U.S. Army Strategic Studies Institute, November 2001, pp. 3-5.

117. This prevalence has been especially noticeable in joint doctrine. In the U.S., the first edition of JP 1 prominently advocated some of the key maneuverist ideas, such as targeting an enemy's strategic and operational centers of gravity. This notion has continued through to the current (2007, incorporating change 1, 2009) edition. The UK, Canada, Australia and New Zealand have been even more explicit, and their joint capstone manuals have all emphasized that their armed forces jointly apply a maneuverist approach. Joint Chiefs of Staff, U.S. Department of Defense, JP 1, 1991, pp. 46, 56, 65; Joint Chiefs of Staff, U.S. Department of Defense, JP 1 *Doctrine for the Armed Forces of the United States,* May 2, 2007, Incorporating Change 1, March 20, 2009, p. I-18, available from *www.dtic.mil/doctrine/new_pubs/jp1.pdf*, accessed on March 4, 2011; British Armed Forces, JWP 0-01, 1st ed., pp. 4.8-4.9; Canadian Forces, Canadian Forces Joint Publication (CFJP) 01 *Canadian Military Doctrine*, 1st ed., Ottawa, ON: Canadian Forces Experimentation Centre, April 2009, pp. 6-13, available from *www.cfd-cdf.forces.gc.ca/cfwc-cgfc/Index/JD/Pub_Eng/ Capstone/ CFJP_%2001_Canadian_Military_Doctrine_En_2009_04_Web.pdf*, accessed on March 4, 2011; Australian Defence Force, ADDP-D *Foundations of Australian Military Doctrine*, 1st ed., Canberra: Defence Publishing Service, May 2002, pp. 5.3-5.5; New Zealand Defence Force, New Zealand Defence Doctrine Publication-Doctrine (NZDDP-D) *Foundations of New Zealand Military Doctrine*, 1st ed., Wellington: Development Branch, Headquarters New Zealand Defence Force, 2004, pp. 6.18-6.19.

118. Strachan, "Operational Art in Britain," pp. 96-136.

119. Romjue, "The Evolution of the AirLand Battle Concept".

Chapter 3

The Relationship between the Four Schools

By the end of the 20th century, four distinct schools of doctrinal ontology had emerged within English speaking western militaries. Before proceeding to discuss the epistemology underlying these schools and the impact of the developments of the early 21st century, it is first pertinent to reflect on the nature of the relationship between these schools. This relationship is important as it situates the emergence of each school within its broader intellectual context while concurrently allowing for the conduct of a detailed analysis of the significance of each in relation to the others.

In this chapter, the relationship between the schools is analyzed from three different perspectives: the educational, the scientific, and the bureaucratic. These perspectives are adopted because each sheds light on a different aspect of the military's institutional belief system as it is expressed within doctrine and together these perspectives also explore the range and significance of the relationships between doctrine, strategy, the military and its environment. It is subsequently determined that despite the differences between each of the four ontological schools, doctrine has nevertheless consistently employed ontological **realism** as the basis of its discourse. This has formed an enduring bond between each of the schools of doctrinal ontology and has usually ensured that they remain mutually compatible despite the different scope of their focus.

The Training and Educational Role of Doctrine

The first of these perspectives relates primarily to the role of doctrine in the delivery of professional military training and education (the difference between training and education is that training is designed to teach a skill whereas education is designed to increase the recipient's knowledge).[1]

As asserted above, each school of doctrinal ontology has been applied in a different manner—as instruction manuals, training aids, guidance, and as an instrument for analysis, respectively. Of note, these applications correspond to the requirements of a military practitioner's professional training and education at various stages of their career trajectory, as identified by Alan Okros within his paper addressing alternative approaches to understanding leadership within a military context.[2]

A brief overview of the relevant aspects of Okros' paper is thus warranted. At the core of his observations about military career progression is the assertion that:

Entry level formation…is based on engineering and the assumptions that one is to focus on learning how to apply known procedures to address the profession's (tactical) issues. Mid-level Officer…and senior [non-commissioned member]… formation is based on the natural sciences and the assumption that, at this level, one must learn how to develop general (operational) plans of action and update existing (tactical) procedures through some form of structured analysis (the Operational Planning Process dominates). Senior level Officer [formation is] based on the liberal arts and the assumption that, at the most senior level, one must learn how to analyze complex issues to establish (strategic) guidance which, in turn, informs operational planning.[3]

This is closely related to the division between long-established modes of general education: "Arts teaches one how to ask the right questions (the strategic focus), the Natural Sciences teach one how to answer these questions the right way (the operational focus), and Engineering teaches one how to apply the answers the right way (the tactical focus)."[4] As a result:

The significant challenge identified is that individuals have to transit across all three major faculties of engineering, sciences, and the arts while also expanding their focus from mastery of the military arena…[to] the full spectrum of government objectives… the key conclusion is that those moving to the most senior staff roles also need to move away from predominant reliance on engineering models based on the assumptions of a knowable, definable, programmable world to adopting philosophical models that acknowledge that one rarely gets the question right let alone determines the answers with absolute certainty.[5]

Importantly, the relationship between each of the successive schools of doctrinal ontology identified above aligns with the training and educational requirements of the military career progression path identified by Okros.

Throughout one's military career, doctrine in the technical manual school is consulted to provide instructions about the employment specific systems. Manuals in this school thus enable training to be conducted with the intent of teaching military practitioners the technical skills they need to do their job. Although technical manuals are more likely to be of relevance to those employed in technical trades (such as artillery or engineers) or to those in the initial stages of their career, there may nevertheless be cause for those at any stage of their career to "consult the instruction manual" if required. Thus, doctrine manuals in this school form a foundation for training throughout one's career.

In alignment with Okros' analogy, doctrine in the tactical manual school can be viewed primarily as a training aid for military "engineers." This doctrine is produced with the underlying assumption that the problems confronting tactical forces are knowable, definable and, to an extent, programmable (regardless of how frequently "re-programming" may be required). Accordingly, the employment of this doctrine as a training aid aligns with the requirements of training military practitioners using an engineering approach.

Doctrine in the other two schools assists in the delivery of education, rather than in the conduct of training. Continuing with Okros' analogy, doctrine in the operational manual school is targeted at an audience of military "natural scientists." In the words of R. K. Taylor, it "is more about creating a framework within which to prepare, plan, and conduct operations…rather than [establishing] procedures on 'how to fight'."[6] For this reason, the guidance it provides can be construed as a means of establishing the appropriate questions that operational planners should seek to answer.

Finally, as it constitutes an instrument for analysis, doctrine in the military strategic school can be interpreted as a component of attempts to determine which ontological questions militaries need to ask. Doctrine manuals in this school therefore constitute something akin to academic textbooks for military "arts" students who (to again paraphrase Okros) are required to analyze a myriad of complex problems as they arise, determine their own creative solutions and while in the process of doing so, define which questions need to be answered. To this end the philosophies, principles, and concepts contained in doctrine manuals that fit within this school fill two roles. In the first, they are an expression of thought about the nature of the strategic questions confronting militaries, and in the second, they are an important source of intellectual support to which military practitioners can refer when justifying why they have determined to ask certain questions. Coincidentally, this latter role corresponds to the citation by arts students of texts that support the hypotheses of their papers.

From the training and educational perspective, it can be seen that the emergence of each school of doctrinal ontology roughly corresponds with major developments in the expansion of formalized professional military training and education programs. As previously mentioned, the publication of "the first modern drill book," *Wapenhandlingen van Roers, Musqetten ende Spiessen*, the year after the establishment of the first modern military academy, is a noteworthy coincidence.[7] The 17th century subsequently witnessed the proliferation within Europe of both military academies and drill manuals, the forerunners to doctrine in the technical manual school. During this period, military academies focused almost exclusively on providing training for the technically inclined military trades of artillery and engineering.[8]

Towards the end of the 18th century, however, many European military academies began to expand their curriculums to cover a broader range of subjects, including military theory and tactics.[9] In the late 18th and early 19th centuries, staff colleges—designed to provide further education for mid-level officers selected to serve in staff appointments—were also opened across the Occident.[10] During the latter half of the 20th century too, formal education programs were expanded or consolidated at all stages of military career progression. This included the establishment in 1983 of the US Army's School of Advanced Military Studies which "offered a rigorous education in the tactical and operational levels of warfare, staff procedures, planning, and problem solving" based on the ontology made explicit in the previous year's edition of Field Manual (FM) 100-5 *Operations*.[11] Alongside these changes is the trend in most English speaking militaries towards an ever increasing percentage of officers holding tertiary or even postgraduate degrees.

The Relationship between Doctrine and Scientific Regimes

The second perspective from which the relationship between the schools of doctrinal ontology can be analyzed is the scientific perspective. In conducting this analysis, the work of Antoine Bousquet is most useful. Conducting "enquiry into the profound interrelationship of science and warfare," Bousquet determined that "throughout the modern era the dominant corpus of scientific ideas has been reflected in the contemporary theories and practices of warfare in the Western world."[12] Furthermore, he posited the existence of:

> four distinct regimes of the scientific way of warfare, each of which is characterised [sic] by a specific theoretical and methodological constellation: mechanistic, thermodynamic,

cybernetic, and chaoplexic warfare. At the core of every scientific regime we find an associated paradigmatic technology, respectively the clock, the engine, the computer, and the network.[13]

Just as the different requirements of professional military education at successive stages of a military career, as identified by Okros, align with the different schools of doctrinal ontology, so too do each of the four "regimes" identified by Bousquet.[14]

The first of these regimes, the mechanistic, was dominant throughout the 17th and 18th centuries. Employing clockwork as its primary technological metaphor, the dominance of this regime was marked by general belief that, in a similar manner to the sequence of interaction between a series of weights as well as cogs and springs within a clock, the world could be holistically understood through an examination of the nature of its component parts and the interaction between them.[15] Alongside the dominance of this regime emerged the first school of doctrinal ontology. Indeed, Bousquet observes about *Wapenhandlingen van Roers, Musqetten ende Spiessen* that it:

> acted as an "integrated instructional device," breaking down the use of any given weapon into a series of distinct component steps which were arranged in a numbered logical sequence and each associated with an individual verbal command. The sequence formed a complete cycle to be repeated as many times as required.[16]

This sequence is, of course, analogous to the sequence of interaction between the components of a clockwork mechanism. Notably, doctrine manuals in the technical manual school have continued to tend towards this methodology right up to present day. The US Army's training revolution of the early 1970s employed the same sequence but on a larger scale, for example.[17]

The second regime, the thermodynamic, assumed primacy during the 19th century, maintained this position until at least the mid-20th century, and employed the engine as its own primary technological metaphor. According to this metaphor, the world is composed of different types of energies that interact with one another and which can be harnessed, concentrated, discharged, or transformed, in the same way that an engine converts its fuel source into motive power through the process of thermodynamics. For militaries, the spread of technologies that had been developed through the application of the science of thermodynamics irreversibly changed war and new technologies such as railways, steamships, automobiles, breech-loading and rifled weapon systems, and eventually airplanes, were all developed as a result of this branch of scientific endeavor.[18]

The period of primacy of this scientific regime also coincided with the emergence of the second school of doctrinal ontology. Assessed from the scientific perspective, it can be concluded that doctrine in this school has indeed been influenced by thermodynamics. In concentrating its discussion on battlefield tactics, it at least tacitly acknowledges the influence of different energies, their interactions, and their exertions and impacts upon one another. In particular, linguistics and metaphors relating to thermodynamics abound. The 1941 edition of FM 100-5, for example, discussed attack and defense in relation to a "war of movement," a concept that is inherently related to the expenditure and transformation of energy.[19]

It is important to note at this juncture that the emergence of new scientific regimes and their ascendency as the dominant paradigm of their era has not been accompanied by the consignment of previous regimes to history. Instead, older regimes have continued to coexist alongside the newer ones, albeit having passed the mantle of dominance, and have even in some instances assumed a complementary position alongside their successors.[20] The same could be said about the influence of each regime on the major concepts that have been featured in doctrine. Hence, mechanistic ideas, such as the "linear battlefield," continued to exist alongside other (newer and hence more prominent) ideas belonging to more recent scientific regimes, long after the mechanistic sciences had ceased to constitute the dominant regime.[21] The same can subsequently be observed in the case of thermodynamics and so on.

The third scientific regime Bousquet identified is the cybernetic and its dominant metaphor is the computer, an apparatus designed to capture information from its environment, process it, and then transmit the results back into the environment thus potentially creating a "feedback loop." This regime has its origins in the technological developments of the Second World War and became a dominant scientific paradigm during the decades thereafter.[22] The key significance of this regime is that "the promises of cybernetic warfare fuelled the dream of a complete automated dominance of the battlefield." This dream soon came to be accompanied by "a drive for certainty and predictability" during military operations.[23]

The influence of this drive on military thought was evident in the development of several new concepts. Most notable is the replacement of the term "command" with "command and control," the latter part of which "suggests a process that involves a feedback mechanism allowing the controller to obtain new information from the system, adjust orders accordingly, and thus exert continuous direction on subordinates" in the same way that a computer captures and processes and then disseminates processed information.[24] Although this regime had already begun to have a noticeable influence on doctrine prior to the emergence of the third school of doctrinal ontology (for instance, the training revolution of the 1970s can be construed from this perspective as employing doctrine as part of a large scale information gathering and processing activity), it nevertheless became an instant feature of the third school doctrine manuals of its era of dominance.

This influence was subtle, however. The 1982 edition of FM 100-5 is illustrative. Despite prominently discussing command and control and addressing the employment and effect of several cybernetic technologies such as sensors and electronic warfare, the cybernetic regime was not immediately evident in most of the content of this manual.[25] Instead, the application of training regimes based on the AirLand Battle concept it featured were the most prominent result of the influence of cybernetics. The Army's National Training Center (NTC), which opened in 1982:

> employed laser weapons to precisely calibrate the damage (so that a rifle could not destroy a tank) and teams of observers to conduct immediate on-site seminars. Cameras and computers recorded the words and actions of individuals and units engaged in combat against a surrogate Soviet force (the Krasnovians). Armor, mechanized, and even light units rotated through the NTC, conducting tactical exercises (or missions) that simulated the violent and intensive combat environment expected in a war with the Soviets.[26]

The application of doctrine had thus taken on the features of an enormous scale cybernetic feedback loop, in which information about performance could be collected, analyzed, assessed, and evaluated and the results widely communicated within a very short timeframe.

The final regime is termed "chaoplexity" by Bousquet in a deliberate amalgamation of the terms "chaos theory" and "complexity science," the two dominant scientific paradigms underlying it.[27] These paradigms emphasize non-linearity and self-organization, and the key metaphor accompanying them is the network, an abstract concept emphasizing multifaceted interaction through an intricate web of interconnectivity that exists between different elements of a system, and between the system and its environment. Relative to the other regimes, chaoplexity is still in a state of intellectual adolescence, having emerged in the sciences during the early 1970s and only beginning to shape military thinking two decades later.[28]

Like cybernetics, chaoplexity has influenced the development of some key military concepts, although its influence has been notably less prominent than any of the other regimes probably due to its relatively short lineage. One of the most prolific concepts identified as employing the principles of chaos theory is John Boyd's Decision Cycle (also known as the Observe-Orient-Decide-Act Cycle or simply as the "OODA loop"), which presents a cognitive model of the decision making process of participants in combat.[29] Bousquet observes a tendency, however, for cybernetic concepts to be construed as chaoplexic when they in fact are not (his highly detailed critique of Network Centric Warfare is informative as it demonstrates this tendency in the case of that concept)[30] or for chaoplexic concepts to be misinterpreted or over-simplified into a more linear form (Boyd's Decision Cycle itself suffers from this).[31]

Hence, there is still a way to go before chaoplexity is fully established as a dominant paradigm within military thinking regardless of its proliferation in the sciences. The application of chaoplexic thinking within doctrine has nevertheless increased in recent years particularly within doctrine in the fourth school. Furthermore, some prominent concepts have been reinterpreted as employing chaoplexic metaphors. One example is the maneuverist approach. In this case, while it is acknowledged that key associated terms such as "friction," "tempo" and "firepower" remain connotative of thermodynamics, the discussion of other ideas such as "uncertainty," "disorder," and even "complexity" clearly demonstrates the presence of chaoplexic modes of interpretation.[32] The rise of this mode of thinking within doctrine will be revisited from an epistemological perspective in the next chapter.

Overall, from the scientific perspective it can be seen that each of the four scientific regimes identified by Bousquet has had a substantial influence on the development of concepts featured within the doctrine produced during the period of its epoch and that each of the regimes has left a noticeable conceptual legacy thereafter. As the emergence of each of the schools of doctrinal ontology has coincided with the dominance of a different scientific regime, the scientific undercurrents of the doctrine in each school can be seen to have expanded from the last. In light of this, it is possible to determine the existence an ongoing relationship between the progress of scientific endeavor on one hand and the content of doctrine on the other.

Doctrine, Military Bureaucracy, and State/Military Relations

The third perspective from which the relationship between the schools of doctrinal ontology can be analyzed is the bureaucratic perspective. Unlike the educational and scientific perspectives, analysis from the bureaucratic perspective is not linked to the writings of any particular individual. Instead, analysis from the bureaucratic perspective draws on various examinations of the rise and expansion of the modern state. It is posited that through this lens the expansion of doctrine can be seen to have paralleled crucial changes in the nature of the states that sustain modern military forces.

The emergence of the modern state, and for that matter of the state-centric international system in which modern militaries purport to operate, is contentious and alternate dates have been suggested. While those attempting to specify a precise date often cite the proclamation of the Peace of Westphalia in 1648,[33] others have argued that a gradual evolution of the modern state occurred from the early 15th to the early 18th century.[34] Regardless of which of these views one accepts, the modern state and the state-centric international system are both underpinned by the primacy of state sovereignty. Although the enshrining of this was a major component of the Peace of Westphalia, this does not mean that the modern state appeared overnight following its proclamation.[35]

Subsequent to its emergence as the primary political unit within the international system, the role of the state has progressively expanded in relation to society. As George Thomas and John Meyer expound, this expansion can be viewed as a mixture of the growth of jurisdiction, rationalization, and bureaucracy linked to an accelerating rate of institutionalization. The first of these facets includes the states' early development of legal systems and taxation structures, the expanding scope of these, and more recently constructed apparatus such as national finance systems, citizens and civil rights, and the regulation of social activities. This has gone hand-in-hand with increasing rationalization, which Thomas and Meyer define as "the organization of social life within a unified frame of means and ends."[36]

Bureaucracy has been the preferred mechanism for controlling the relationship between means and ends associated with increasing rationalization and for implementing the requirements of increasing jurisdiction. The increased scope and size of bureaucratic mechanisms in particular has been one of the most immediately visible elements of state expansion. Accompanying this has been an accelerating rate of institutionalization within Western society. In the latter half of the 20th century, for example, this encompassed most prominently the expansion of public education and state-provided welfare mechanisms, closely linked to shifting conceptions of citizens' rights in relation to state-provided services.[37]

Although they offer an excellent summary of the key elements of state-expansion, Thomas and Meyer's account approaches the subject from a sociological rather than historical perspective. Hence, it remains somewhat ahistoric and a greater elaboration of a few key events is required.

The period following the Peace of Westphalia was dominated by the monarchic governance of European states, by the occurrence of "limited wars" and by the expansion of European power into newly-established colonies. The practice of warfare during this period remained limited to the conduct of war by permanent "volunteer" military forces that were officered primarily by members of the aristocracy. The role, scope, and *modus operandi* of the state and its institutions evolved slowly throughout this period, at least relatively to those preceding and following it.[38] This was also the period in which the first school of doctrinal ontology emerged.

The revolutions in North America from 1774 to 1783 and France from 1789 to 1799 brought fundamental changes to the relationship between states and society. In particular, the concept of citizenship was drastically altered. After the revolutions, citizenship became universal and a new relationship between "the people" and the state was established wherein the people were subjected to increased state jurisdiction in exchange for an increased stake in the state itself.[39] This new relationship spread across Europe during the 19th century witnessed by increased nationalism on the part of the people and by increased jurisdiction, rationalization, and bureaucracy on the part of the state. It was against this backdrop that the vast conscripted European militaries that would eventually contest both World Wars emerged and that these militaries concurrently professionalized and bureaucratized.[40] It was also against this backdrop that the second school of doctrinal ontology first appeared.

Gradual expansion of the state continued into the 20th century, accelerating during the decades following the Second World War. As mentioned above, this encompassed most prominently the expansion of public education and welfare mechanisms as popular notions of citizens' rights again expanded during this period. This is related to the expanding concept of human rights that was traditionally confined to civil and political rights (such as those granted by the Bill of Rights enshrined within the US Constitution), but which has more recently expanded to include economic rights (such as freedom from poverty and access to education) and social and cultural rights (to ensure the protection of culture and identity).[41] As citizens have come to expect states to uphold these additional rights, state jurisdiction has increased as has rationalization and bureaucracy, and institutionalization has greatly expanded within areas such as education and welfare.[42] English speaking Western militaries, now only one state institution amongst several, during this period have further professionalized and bureaucratized, and have returned to a voluntary model of service.[43]

Turning to the relationship between states and militaries, it is noteworthy that modern militaries have existed as a recognizable institution since the 16th century, about the same time that the modern state itself came to exist.[44] The evolution of these two entities is inextricably linked, with militaries constituting one of the oldest institutions of the state. While still a newly-emerged institution, militaries naturally began to develop their own institutional discourse, which consisted of written as well as other elements. In light of state expansion and the growth of bureaucracy in particular, the widening scope of written doctrine can be viewed as the gradual bureaucratization of the military's dominant institutional discourse.

Just as the appearance of the first and second schools of doctrinal ontology coincided with certain key aspects of state emergence and expansion, so too did the third and fourth. The singular explicit ontology of doctrine in the third school can be viewed as the translation into writing of what had, by the latter part of the 20th century, become the dominant idealized model of the state/military relationship.[45] In this relationship, militaries exist within the international arena and their purpose is to deter or defeat the conventional military forces of other states.[46]

The circumstance of the emergence of this school is significant. The US Army, where this school of doctrinal ontology originated (at least within English speaking militaries), had recently emerged from a guerrilla war against an unconventional enemy force, was seeking to refocus itself on what it considered to be its core business,[47] and was also attempting to address major challenges to its hitherto longstanding institutional and bureaucratic norms.[48] By making its dominant institutional ontology explicit in writing, the Army's jurisdiction as a bureaucratic organization and subset of the state was clearly defined and its legitimacy within American society resultantly increased (or, perhaps more accurately, was restored to something akin to its pre-Vietnam status). The US Army's success in this regard may partially explain the subsequent spread of this school to other military organizations, which sought to emulate its success.

In the period following the Cold War, the ontology defined within the third school was challenged both by the removal of the Soviet military threat to the West and by the proliferation of military activities other than conventional war. As they were called upon to undertake an increasing variety of activities including most notably peace enforcement missions and the provision of humanitarian assistance, English speaking western militaries were also challenged by post-Cold War budgetary pressures.[49] Not only were the perceived role of military institutions and their jurisdiction in relation to that of the state shifting but the military bureaucracy was coming under increasing pressure from the state to justify its ongoing institutional legitimacy.[50] In this environment, there was a need for the military to again expand the scope of its institutional discourse and doctrine in the fourth school emerged to fill the void.

Viewed from the bureaucratic perspective, it can thus be determined that each of the schools of doctrinal ontology emerged either as a result of state expansion (the first and second) or because militaries— understood to be bureaucratic institutions of the state—were acting to either increase or maintain their legitimacy (the third and fourth). It is therefore unsurprising that the expansion of the modern state, of modern military institutions, and of the scope of written doctrine, has occurred concomitantly.

Doctrine and Ontological Realism

When examined together, the educational, scientific, and bureaucratic perspectives reveal that the relationship between the schools of doctrinal ontology is complicated and multifaceted. Returning to the definition of doctrine given at the opening of this monograph—that doctrine is the most visible expression of a military's belief system—it can now be concluded that this belief system has been shaped by an interwoven mixture of trends that are inherent within western society itself. It is further evident that the ontology underlying written doctrine (and for that matter whether doctrine has taken written or verbal form) is related to the institutional evolution of modern militaries. Changes in doctrinal taxonomies have resulted from, and have in turn influenced, concurrent military expansion, professionalization, and bureaucratization. The nature of these changes has been strongly influenced by emerging technologies and by dominant scientific and sociological paradigms.

It is worth pausing at this juncture also to recall that ontology is the examination of the nature of being and of the first principles—or categories—involved. It is concerned with the formulation of taxonomies that enable an understanding of relationships between objects to be reached. Analysis to this point has established the existence of four distinct ontological schools of doctrine, has discussed the taxonomies identified within each, and has elaborated the significance of their evolution in relation to broader trends.

Before moving onto the next chapter, a final observation about ontology is required. The difference between each of the four schools of doctrinal ontology is evident most clearly in the scope of their content, which incrementally, but also greatly, expands between the first and fourth schools. Despite this difference, it is also noteworthy that all of the schools have traditionally been linked by the single ontological assumption that reality exists, regardless of how individuals may perceive (or fail to perceive) its existence. Because of this, doctrine is fundamentally **realist**—an ontological perspective that emphasizes that the world beyond human cognition is structured and tangible regardless of whether or not humans perceive and label it. This perspective is often contrasted with **nominalism,** which emphasizes that the identification and labeling of structures is fundamentally necessary for establishing their existence. Without labels, reality remains unstructured.[51]

The appeal of ontological realism to militaries is understandable. Military practitioners are frequently required to venture into harm's way where they may be hurt or even killed regardless of whether they understand, or have labeled, the relationships they are encountering.[52] This notwithstanding, militaries are prolific labelers and the concepts featured in doctrine can be viewed as a means of labeling objects, structures, and the relationships between them. Given the military tendency to ontological realism, this is done not to create reality but in an effort to come to an understanding of how it works, the ultimate aim being to subsequently manipulate it in order to achieve a desired outcome (victory).

Notes

1.   Thomas E. Sheets, *"Training" and "Educating" Marine Corps Officers for the Future*, unpublished monograph: U.S. Army War College, April 1992, pp. 4-6, available from *http://www.dtic.mil/dtic/tr/fulltext/u2/a249432.pdf*, accessed on September 30, 2012.

2.   Alan Okros, *Leadership in the Canadian Military Context*, Canadian Forces Leadership Institute Monograph 2010-01, Canada: Canadian Forces Leadership Institute, November 2010.

3.   In this context, Okros uses the term "formation" to refer to both an individual's official education and training, and to the accompanying informal process of socialization. Okros, p. 39.

4.   Okros, *Leadership in the Canadian Military Context*, p. 39.

5.   Okros, *Leadership in the Canadian Military Context*, pp. 40-1.

6.   R. K. Taylor, "2020 Vision: Canadian Forces Operational-Level Doctrine," *Canadian Military Journal*, Vol. 2, No. 3, Autumn 2001, pp. 35-42.

7.   John Childs, "The Military Revolution I: The Transition to Modern Warfare," in Charles Townshend, ed, *The Oxford Illustrated History of Modern War*, Oxford: Oxford University Press, 1997, pp. 32-33.

8.   Martin van Creveld, *The Training of Officers: From Military Professionalism to Irrelevance*, New York, NY: The Free Press, 1990, pp. 13-16. The early history U.S. Military Academy at West Point presents another example of this tendency. See: Russell F. Weigley, "American Strategy from its Beginnings through the First World War," in Paret, ed., *Makers of Modern Strategy*, pp. 413-8.

9.   Azar Gat, *A History of Military Thought: From the Enlightenment to the Cold War*, Oxford: Oxford University Press, 2001, Bk II, pp. 285-6. English speaking militaries too followed this pattern. In the United Kingdom, the Royal Military Academy at Woolwich, which delivered training for Royal Engineers and Royal Artillery officers, was inaugurated in 1741. Yet it was not until 1801 that the Royal Military College was opened, offering a course for future officers of less technical trades, primarily cavalry and infantry. Similarly, the opening of the U.S. Military Academy at West Point in 1802 was preceded by the establishment in 1794 of a more limited course teaching engineering and artillery topics. Anthony Clayton, *The British Officer: Leading the Army from 1660 to the Present,* Edinburgh Gate: Pearson Education, 2007, pp. 57-58, 72, 88; Brian McAllister Linn, *The Echo of Battle: The Army's Way of War*, Cambridge, MA: Harvard University Press, 2007, p. 11.

10.   The forerunner to these military institutes of "higher education" was established within France's Ministry of War during the 1780s. The establishment of staff colleges in other European militaries was a gradual and erratic process, with the last major European power to open such a college being Russia in 1832. Van Creveld, *The Training of Officers*, pp. 17-67.

11. Linn, *The Echo of Battle*, p. 212.

12. Antoine Bousquet, *The Scientific Way of Warfare: Order and Chaos on the Battlefields of Modernity,* London: Hurst and Co., 2009, p. 3.

13. Bousquet, *The Scientific Way of Warfare,* p. 4.

14. Deferring to Fritjof Capra, Bousquet defines a "regime" as a "social paradigm," which is understood to be "a constellation of concepts, values, perceptions, and practices shared by a community, which forms a particular vision of reality that is the basis of the way the community organizes itself." Capra, quoted in Bousquet, *The Scientific Way of Warfare,* p. 13. Of note, this definition is somewhat similar to Fleck's concept of "thought communities," as applied by Coombs (see: Coombs, "In the Wake of a Paradigm Shift", p. 25). Both of these concepts are revisited in the fifth chapter.

15. Bousquet, *The Scientific Way of Warfare,* pp. 37-43.

16. Bousquet, *The Scientific Way of Warfare,* p. 58.

17. Linn, *The Echo of Battle*, pp. 200-1.

18. Bousquet, *The Scientific Way of Warfare*, pp. 64-85.

19. U.S. Army, FM 100-5 *Field Service Regulations: Operations* [first issued 1941]. Ft Leavenworth: U.S. Army Command and General Staff College Press, 1992, pp. 112-6.

20. Bousquet, *The Scientific Way of Warfare.*

21. The conceptualization of the battlefield as linear appeared frequently in doctrine manuals in the second school right up until the latter third of the 20th century. On the origins of the linear conceptualization of warfare, see: Lynn, *Battle*, chap. 4. Significantly, establishing that the battlefield is non-linear was at the forefront of the first manual in the third ontological school. Headquarters, Department of the Army, FM 100-5 *Operations*, Washington DC: U.S. Government Printing Office, August 20, 1982, pp. 1.1-1.2.

22. Bousquet, *The Scientific Way of Warfare*, pp. 93-119.

23. Bousquet, *The Scientific Way of Warfare,* p. 126.

24. Bousquet, *The Scientific Way of Warfare,* pp. 128-9.

25. Headquarters, Department of the Army, FM 100-5, 1982, pp. 7.3-7.7.

26. Linn, *The Echo of Battle*, p. 215.

27. Bousquet has borrowed this term from the earlier work of John Horgan. See: Bousquet, *The Scientific Way of Warfare*, p. 164.

28. One of the earliest examples of the implications of this paradigm being considered from a strategic studies perspective is: Steven R. Mann, "Chaos Theory and Strategic Thought," *Parameters*, Vol. XXII, No. 3, Autumn 1992, pp. 54-68.

29. Bousquet, *The Scientific Way of Warfare*, pp. 187-96. For details of Boyd's Decision Cycle, see: Frans P. B. Osinga, *Science, Strategy and War: The Strategic Theory of John Boyd,* London: Routledge, 2007. Although the conceptual development of the Decision Cycle is revisited throughout, pp. 229-32 are particularly pertinent. Boyd's own graphical representation of the Cycle is reproduced on p. 231.

30. Bousquet, *The Scientific Way of Warfare.*

31. "The idea that victory depends on getting inside the enemy's OODA 'loop' has become commonplace in contemporary military literature, particularly in the network-centric variety, to the extent that it has become something of an incantation that is not always based on a consistent and faithful understanding of Boyd's ideas." Bousquet, *The Scientific Way of Warfare*, pp. 194-5. See also: Osinga, *Science, Strategy and War*, pp. 5-6, which makes a similar criticism.

32. All of these terms have been sourced from: Headquarters, U.S. Marine

Corps, Marine Corps Doctrine Publication (MCDP) 1 *Warfighting,* Washington DC: U.S. Government Printing Office, June 20, 1997.

33. See discussion in: Kalevi J. Holsti, *Peace and War: Armed Conflicts and International Order 1648-1989*, Cambridge Studies in International Relations No. 14, Cambridge: Cambridge University Press, 1991, pp. 25-42.

34. Martin Wight, *Systems of States,* Leicester, UK: Leicester University Press, 1977, pp. 129-152.

35. Bruce D. Porter's account presents a typical assessment: "The peace of Westphalia is often viewed as marking the birth of the modern European state system and the formal recognition of the concept of state sovereignty but this is far more evident in retrospect than it was at the time…The Thirty Years' War did not render Europe modern overnight, but it accelerated the modernizing forces already unleashed by the Military Revolution and the Reformation." Bruce D. Porter, *War and the Rise of the State: The Military Foundations of Modern Politics*, New York, NY: The Free Press, 1994, p. 72.

36. George M. Thomas & John W. Meyer, "The Expansion of the State," *Annual Review of Sociology*, No. 10, 1984, pp. 468-70, quote p. 469.

37. Thomas & Meyer, pp. 470-7.

38. Porter, *War and the Rise of the State*, pp. 105-21.

39. Charles Tilly, *Coercion, Capital, and European States, AD 990-1992,* Oxford: Blackwell, 1992, pp. 107-114; Porter, *War and the Rise of the State*, pp. 121-37, 243-57.

40. Porter, *War and the Rise of the State*, pp. 149-193.

41. These different types of rights have been labeled first, second and third generation rights. See: Anthony J. Langlois, "Human Rights," in Martin

Griffiths, ed., *Encyclopedia of International Relations and Global Politics,*
Abingdon: Routledge, 2006, pp. 385-93.

42. Thomas & Meyer, "The Expansion of the State," pp. 475-7.

43. Hal Klepak, "Some Reflections on Generalship Through the Ages," in
Bernd Horn & Stephen J. Harris, eds., *Generalship and the Art of the Admiral:
Perspectives on Canadian Senior Military Leadership*, St. Catherines, ON:
Vanwell Publishing, 2001, pp. 32-3.

44. Childs, "The Military Revolution I," pp. 21-2.

45. Eliot A. Cohen, *Supreme Command: Soldiers, Statesmen and
Leadership in Wartime*, New York: The Free Press, 2002, pp. 225-9.

46. Cohen, *Supreme Command,* pp. 225-9.

47. Conrad C. Crane, *Avoiding Vietnam: The U.S. Army's Response to
Defeat in Southeast Asia*, Carlisle, PA: U.S. Army Strategic Studies Institute,
September 2002, p. 17.

48. The most fundamental of these was the institutional shift from a con-
script-based to a volunteer force; however, the concurrent need to address major
morale, discipline and drug problems constituted major bureaucratic challenges
as well. Roger J. Spiller, "In the Shadow of the Dragon: Doctrine and the U.S.
Army after Vietnam," in Jeffrey Grey & Peter Dennis, eds., *From Past to
Future: The Australian Experience of Land/Air Operations*, Canberra: Australian
Defence Force Academy, 1995, pp. 15-6.

49. John Allen Williams, "The Postmodern Military Reconsidered," in
Charles C. Moskos, John Allen Williams & David R. Segal, eds., *The Postmodern
Military: Armed Forces After the Cold War,* New York, NY: Oxford University
Press, 2000, pp. 267-8.

50. Williams, pp.265-7.

51. Gibson Burrell & Gareth Morgan, *Sociological Paradigms and
Organisational Analysis: Elements of the Sociology of Corporate Life*,
Portsmouth: Heinemenn, 1979, p. 4.

52. A detailed study of the ontological perspectives and assumptions of military
practitioners is absent from the existing literature. As a consequence of this void, the
assertion made here is based on a dual assessment from an ontological perspective
of the content and application of doctrine, and of existing studies of military and
Service culture. Works addressing the latter include: Carl H. Builder *The Masks
of War: American Military Styles in Strategy and Analysis,* Baltimore, MD: John
Hopkins University Press, 1989; Allan D. English, *Understanding Military Culture:
A Canadian Perspective,* Montreal, QC: McGill-Queens University Press, 2004.

Chapter 4

The Epistemology of Doctrine

Having now explored the nature of doctrinal ontology, this monograph shifts its focus to the epistemology of doctrine. To this end, the first section of this chapter determines that **positivism**, an approach characterized by (self-proclaimed) rationality and objectivity, has provided the epistemological foundation of doctrine for the first 400 years of its existence. As such, examples of positivist approaches abound within doctrine and include most measurable, quantifiable, or linear processes, such as that used to determine when a soldier has qualified on a weapon system or even the military planning process itself.

While positivism remains dominant, since the start of the 21st century **anti-positivism**, emphasizing relativity and subjectivity, has begun to influence doctrine, signaling what is perhaps the most salient change in the nature of written doctrine since its inception. The emergence of this new epistemological approach is chronicled in the second section of this chapter. The third section then discusses the situation that led to the emergence of the most prominent manifestation of this new epistemological approach to date – the "design" concept featured in several recent US Army, Marine Corps, and joint doctrine manuals.

Although anti-positivist approaches have already shaped contemporary operational conduct, the epistemological shift to anti-positivism is still in its infancy and concepts such as design have been the subject of much recent debate. The state of the debate surrounding deign in particular is summarized in the final section of this chapter and from this it becomes clear that anti-positivist approaches have yet to reach their full potential.[1]

Doctrine's "Traditional" Epistemology: Military Positivism

Given the consistency with which doctrine has reflected ontological realism, it is unsurprising that its epistemology also remained constant from the 17th to the 20th centuries. Its epistemological approach is **positivism**, the key aspects of which require explanation. The term "positivism" was coined by philosopher Auguste Comte in the mid-19th century and his work subsequently "played a significant role in shaping the emerging social sciences in the latter half of the 19th century"—the period during which the second school of doctrinal ontology was in its adolescence. The origins of the positivist approach, however, are in the Enlightenment, an intellectual era that ran approximately from the late 17th century to the conclusion of the 18th century.[2]

The key intellectual facets of the Enlightenment were fourfold. First, was the belief that the functioning of the world as a whole, including all of its components regardless of size or consequence, was subject to a single set of overarching laws that could be discovered and understood by man. Second, man was capable of both individual and societal improvement. Third, there were several compatible goals such as justice, happiness, liberty, knowledge, and virtue, which all men sought. Finally, as human progress was possible, these goals were obtainable. That they had not yet been obtained was the result of ignorance of either the goals themselves or the means of achieving them and this ignorance was a product of the failure of man to recognize and understand the universal laws governing the world.[3]

Importantly for the subsequent development of epistemological positivism, the intellectual viewpoint of the Enlightenment established that man was a rational actor, capable of coming to a logical reasoned understanding of the world around him.[4] In making positivism explicit, Comte's determination that valid knowledge could be obtained through a combination of initial observation and subsequent reasoning reveals the link between his outlook and that of the intellectuals of the Enlightenment.[5]

At risk of over-simplification, the methodology advocated by positivism (as developed by Comte as well as numerous subsequent scholars)[6] can be summarized as one in which the subjects of study should be observed from a neutral viewpoint with the results of observation subsequently being assessed in a rational objective manner in order to allow the researcher to determine the universal laws governing the relationships between them. Advocates of positivism, including Comte himself, have asserted that this approach should be applied not only within the natural sciences but also within the social sciences and humanities where the discovery of universal laws would facilitate their subsequent application to selectively alter social conditions so as to bring about desired changes to a society.[7]

The impact of positivism on doctrine development has been described by Christopher Paparone, whose brief typology offers one of the few available examinations of doctrinal epistemology (although he noticeably avoids using the term "epistemology" itself). Asserting that "positivism served the foundation [sic] of traditional, post-WW II US doctrine," he was quick to characterize this doctrine as "focus[ing] on reductionism, empiricism, linearity, mathematical logic, and predictable cause-and-effect relationships."[8] In light of discussion above, it can be determined that his assessment of the temporal and geographical locations of this doctrine was excessively limited – pre-Second World War doctrine also adopted positivist methodology and this methodology was far from limited to the US military.

Basing his analysis on a two-dimensional continual construct featuring endurance (defined as the rate of change required to maintain doctrinal currency over time) on the horizontal axis and exclusivity (determined by the number of concepts featured in a manual) on the vertical, Paparone identified a key difference between what he labeled "highly positivist" and "moderately positivist" doctrine.[9] The key difference between these was their endurance—highly positivist doctrine changed less over time. Both types of doctrine were assessed as being highly exclusive, featuring only a few relatively simple concepts in each manual.

Given the relevance of Paparone's work to this study, cursory though it may have been, it is worth recounting his description of each of these types of doctrine at length. Regarding highly positivist doctrine, he assessed that:

> Doctrinal remedies (like independent variables) for a standing list of problems (like dependent variables) can be expressed in predetermined terms of tasks and standards. For example, doctrine expressing how a Soldier, Sailor, Airman, Marine, or Coast Guardsman (military practitioner) must qualify on his or her assigned weapon can be quite effective...Effectiveness of [highly positivist] doctrine is assessed as much more objective than subjective, using mathematical probabilities and measures of effectiveness...Rule-based, sequential, well-oiled, machine-like command and control works well in executing this type of doctrine...A "trade school" (basic and advanced individual training) approach is suitable for indoctrination of Soldiers in this type.[10]

Although this description clearly applies to doctrine in the first ontological school (Paparone's affiliation of this doctrine with a "trade school" teaching approach is akin to the description herein of first school doctrine as "technical manuals"), Paparone also determined that some of the doctrine assessed by this study as falling within the second school fits the description of highly positivist. For example, "a view of the 1976 edition of Army FM 100-5 [Field Manual 100-5 *Operations*] (the precursor to 3.0) could be categorized as a positivist doctrine focused on simplicity, linearity, and predictability."[11]

Moderately positivist doctrine "is process oriented and requires well-controlled hard-science-like research methods to generate creative hypothesis, identify critical factors (variables), and courses of action as well as plans for contingencies if things do not go as planned."[12] It is based on:

> Rational decision-making processes or templated campaign planning [that] might work well depending on factor analysis of such things as mission, enemy, time and troops available, and terrain and weather... [Moderately positivist] doctrine prescribes processes rather than preset solutions (found in [highly positivist doctrine]) and requires military staff practitioners with specialized and practiced analytical skills where hierarchical (commander-centric) decision making works well...
>
> ...The dominant values that drive this type of doctrine are, like with [highly positivist doctrine], associated primarily with exclusivity; however, practitioners are much more willing to speculate on what can possibly happen outside the conventional organization of "troop-to-task" and perhaps into the interagency realm... moderately positivist approaches call for planned activities driven by forecasted conditions. A "professional school" setting (like the traditional command and general staff college) is appropriate for training and educating Soldiers [to apply] this type [of doctrine]. [13]

This description is applicable to the vast majority of manuals found in the second, third and fourth schools of doctrinal ontology.

That positivism can be identified in doctrine manuals that fit within all four ontological schools, and in countless manuals produced across the span of several centuries, are indicative of the pervasiveness of this branch of epistemology amongst doctrine developers.[14] This in turn is representative of the institutional belief systems of the military forces that develop such doctrine manuals–warranted knowledge is that which can be mathematically measured when a subject is assessed from a neutral viewpoint.

The pervasiveness of doctrinal positivism is evidenced further in the official definition of doctrine employed by many Western militaries, including the US military and its North Atlantic Treaty Organization (NATO) partners. The US definition, for example, is that doctrine constitutes "fundamental principles by which military forces or elements thereof guide their actions in support of national objectives."[15] In this case, it is implied that there can exist a separation between an observer (military practitioner/planner) and a subject (current or future military actions, enemy actions, and/or the environment/situation). The term "fundamental principles," which is noticeably reminiscent of Enlightenment thinking, is particularly important, as it assumes the existence of principles themselves, which the observer (again, the military practitioner/planner) can determine when a subject (past military activities) is assessed from a rational perspective.[16] The addendum to this definition of the caveat that doctrine "is authoritative but requires judgment in application" constitutes a nod to post-Enlightenment intellectual trends.[17] However, this nod does not alter the definition's underlying positivism, as the sound application of judgment presumes the conduct of rational thinking as a prerequisite.

The implications of this intellectual foundation have been the subject of much recent analysis, although this has rarely been undertaken from an epistemological viewpoint. The timing of the growth of this analysis has been driven by two factors. The first is the implications of the emergence of Bousquet's fourth scientific regime or more specifically the growing application of chaos theory and complexity science within doctrine. The second has been a response to the nature of the wars of the early 21st century and the initial failure of doctrine to provide adequate guidance for their prosecution. Both of these factors are explored in depth in the next section but it is nevertheless necessary to mention them here as these motives, particularly the second, provide an explanation as to why much of the recent analysis of doctrinal positivism has viewed that positivism negatively.[18]

For example, in one of the earliest critiques of doctrinal positivism, the argument of which has since been echoed with increasing frequency, Steven R. Mann asserted that:

> The revolution in strategy founded on a mechanistic ordering of reality has been frozen in place and the provocative doctrines of the last century have become the confining dogmas of this one... Not only does classical strategic thought seek to explain conflict in linear, sequential terms, but it compels us to reduce highly complex situations down to a few major variables.[19]

This critique highlights what is perhaps the most significant reason for the widespread adoption within doctrine of a positivist worldview. It posits the existence of determinable cause and effect relationships, provided the variables involved can be identified and, preferably, quantified. In so doing, positivist methodology allows strategists and military theorists (and for that matter doctrine writers) to stipulate formulas that, if conceptually sound and correctly applied, should bring about military victory. Despite the recent criticism the application of positivism within military doctrine has attracted because of this very aspect of its nature, its approach was nevertheless well suited for fighting the increasingly-large scale and industrialized interstate wars that dominated the international system from the time of the Peace of Westphalia until very recently.

Twenty-First Century Doctrine: An Epistemological Shift?

As observed above, the number of critiques of "traditional" military doctrine (that founded in positivist epistemology) has grown in recent years.[20] Generally, these critiques are driven by one (or sometimes both) of two motives: the growing perception of a need to apply chaos theory and complexity science within doctrine; and the initial failure of positivist doctrine to provide adequate guidance for the wars of the early 21st century. Of these motives, the former emerged over a decade before the latter, with the tentative application of chaos and complexity theory to military affairs initially occurring during the late 1980s.[21]

At the crux of the critiques from this perspective is the belief either that the international system is becoming increasingly complex, as is the nature and role of warfare within it, or that we are becoming more aware of its complexity. These critiques emerged to coincide with the end of the Cold War and have become increasingly popular since. Mann's argument has again become typical:

> Traditionally, we see strategic thought as the interplay of a limited number of factors, principally military, economic, and political. More sophisticated discussions expand the set to include factors such as the environment, technological development, and social pressures. Yet even this list fails to convey the full complexity of international affairs…The closer we come to an honest appreciation of the international environment, the more we must confess that it is nonlinear and frustratingly interactive.[22]

Even within the realm of warfare, as opposed to the international system more generally, an increasing level of complexity has been observed in recent decades. Michael Evans, for example, determined that during the 1990s, warfare fractured into three varieties. These he identified as modern (encompassing conventional warfare between states), postmodern (encompassing peacekeeping and humanitarian intervention), and pre-modern (encompassing sub-state and trans-state warfare). While he attributed unique features to each, he also noted that these three varieties of warfare overlap and that the boundaries between them are easily obfuscated.[23]

In response to these observations, as early as the mid-1990s attempts to apply chaos theory can be discerned in a limited array of doctrine manuals, most notably that of the US Marine Corps. In announcing the development of the new series of USMC doctrine manuals in 1996 (the Marine Corps Doctrine Publication (MCDP) series), Lieutenant General Paul K. Van Riper, then Commanding General of the Marine Corps Combat Development Command, asserted that the new series "will not simply codify conventional military wisdom but will expand the boundaries of doctrine by incorporating lessons from other disciplines including the new sciences. Specifically, the manuals will incorporate, as appropriate, the implications of chaos and complexity theory."[24] In particular, the manuals MCDP 1 *Warfighting*, MCDP 1-1 *Strategy* and MCDP 6 *Command and Control* have been credited for incorporating chaos theory and complexity science into USMC doctrine during the mid-1990s.[25] This incorporation was, however, subtle, an approach to introducing new subject matter that was intended to avoid what Christopher Bassford identified as "sales resistance" to the introduction of new paradigms into doctrine.[26]

Counterinsurgency, Design, and Anti-Positivism

Since the onset of the major wars of the 21st century, in particular those in Iraq and Afghanistan, the willingness of military practitioners to accept the introduction of new paradigms into doctrine has markedly increased. This is due mostly to the initial failure of positivist doctrine to provide adequate guidance for the conduct of these wars, an occurrence that brought criticism of earlier modes of doctrinal thinking into the mainstream and which triggered doctrine writers to look for new solutions to military problems.

The story of the emergence and evolution of this criticism has been widely told. Notably, its scale and pervasiveness has been compared to the "doctrinal renaissance" of the early 1980s, which itself had brought about the emergence of the third school of doctrinal ontology. Just as this "renaissance" was the result of the US military experience in Vietnam, the initial criticism of doctrine as ill-suited to the wars of the 21st century grew out of the experience of the early years of the War in Iraq.

As far as most of the popular literature is concerned, the most significant manifestation of this criticism was the development and publication of the 2006 edition of the US Army and Marine Corps *Counterinsurgency* doctrine manual.[27] Although its Army and Marine Corps manual numbers, FM 3-24 and Marine Corps Warfighting Publication (MCWP) 3-33.5

respectively, indicate that this manual occupies a spot in the doctrine hierarchy commensurate with manuals in the second ontological school, the 2006 edition of *Counterinsurgency* incorporates elements of the second, third, and fourth schools and therefore does not sit easily within the extant ontological construct.[28] Why this is the case warrants further attention.

The situation leading to the development of this manual is now a familiar tale. In very brief summary, it begins sometime after the invasion and occupation of Iraq when a small but growing cadre of junior and mid-ranking US Army officers began to publically criticize the US military strategy being used there.[29] At times, this criticism became outright dissent.[30] Soon, this cadre was accompanied by a prominent group of retired general officers who also spoke publically against the US war strategy (this was later dubbed "the revolt of the generals").[31] The core criticism leveled by both of these groups was that the Army was losing the war in Iraq because of its failure to adopt an appropriate counterinsurgency strategy.[32]

A period of further debate as to what might constitute the "right" strategy followed. As the debate widened, an eclectic mix of civilians rose to prominence alongside their military counterparts.[33] By 2006, (then) Lieutenant General David Petraeus, whose tour of duty as Commander of the 101st Airborne Division in Mosul in 2003 has been widely credited as an early example of effective senior command in Iraq, became a key personality within this group.[34] His posting in 2006 as Commander US Army Combined Arms Center gave him an opportunity to put forward an alternative military strategy for waging the war in Iraq.

This strategy was developed in close consultation with several of the officers and civilians who had previously expressed dissenting views about the prosecution of the Iraq war. It also involved an unprecedented level of collaboration between Petraeus and his USMC counterpart, Lieutenant General James Mattis, a cooperation that resulted in the manual being given positions in both the Army and USMC doctrine hierarchies. Updating the *Counterinsurgency* doctrine manual was the primary mechanism used to put forward the strategy with the writing team headed by a retired Army officer-turned-academic, Dr Conrad Crane.[35]

Published in December 2006, the immediate impact of the manual was unprecedented in scale. It was downloaded 1.5 million times in the month after it was posted on the internet by the Army and Marine Corps. It was reviewed in numerous forums that ranged from widely-circulated periodicals such as the *New York Times* to the websites of Jihadist groups.[36] Overall, it may possibly be the best known and widest circulated military doctrine manual ever published.

For the purposes of discussion herein, two components of its content are especially important. The first was a discussion of "social network analysis." Although included in an annex, this discussion was closely linked to the third chapter which addressed the role of intelligence in counterinsurgency operations, stressing the importance of building an understanding the social, economic, cultural, religious, political, ethnic and linguistic aspects of the operating environment as well as conducting more traditional analyses of enemy forces.[37] The annex discussing social network analysis drew heavily on complexity sciences and chaos theory directly engaging with the concept of the *network* that Bousquet had identified as paradigmatic of the fourth regime (chaoplexity) of the "scientific way of warfare."[38] The *Counterinsurgency* manual translated this abstract concept into something more tangible that could be applied by military staffs to help them develop an understanding of societies, cultures, and insurgent groups operating within (and between) them.

Second, the *Counterinsurgency* manual discussed "designing counterinsurgency campaigns and operations" in its fourth chapter. The significance of this is the incorporation of design thinking into doctrine. The chapter defined "design" by contrasting it to traditional military planning:

> Design and planning are qualitatively different yet interrelated activities essential for solving complex problems… Presented a problem, staffs often rush directly into planning without clearly understanding the complex environment of the situation, purpose of military involvement, and approach required to address the core issues… Planning applies established procedures to solve a largely understood problem within an accepted framework. Design inquires into the nature of a problem to conceive a framework for solving that problem. In general, planning is problem solving, while design is problem setting. Where planning focuses on generating a plan, a series of executable actions, design focuses on learning about the nature of an unfamiliar problem.[39]

As Nagl noted in the introduction to the Chicago University Press edition, design was "a gift from the Marine Corps members of the writing team."[40] Although this may have been the case regarding the development of the *Counterinsurgency* manual itself, in fact the term's origin in the military vernacular lies with the Israeli Defence Force (IDF), which developed a Systemic Operational Design (SOD) concept during the 1990s. This concept in turn drew heavily on design thinking and systems theory that had been developed within the social sciences and humanities as far back as the 1940s.[41]

Although the content of the 2006 *Counterinsurgency* manual influenced several aspects of the 2008 edition of FM 3-0 *Operations*,[42] the extent of the spread of design thinking is perhaps more indicative of the *Counterinsurgency* manual's general acceptance within the US military. In addition to discussing design in the 2008 edition of FM 3-0, the Army has included it in the 2008 manual FM 3-07 *Stability Operations* and in the 2010 edition of FM 5-0 *The Operations Process*.[43] Outside of the Army, design has been elaborated in the 2010 edition of MCWP 5-1 *Marine Corps Planning Process*[44] and in the 2011 edition of the joint manual Joint Publication (JP) 5-0 *Joint Operation Planning*.[45] The inclusion of discussions about design thinking in this variety of publications, especially JP 5-0, indicates the concept's institutional acceptance by the US military.

From an epistemological perspective, the inclusion of social network analysis and design thinking within doctrine (as well as the USMC's earlier discussion of chaos theory within certain manuals in the MCDP series) signal a move away from doctrine's traditional positivism and towards an approach more akin to **anti-positivism**. Refuting the core methodology underlying positivism—i.e. objective assessment of the subject of study based on observation from a neural perspective—anti-positivism instead determines that there can be no such thing as an "observer" when studying social phenomena (which include warfare, strategy, and most other areas of military endeavor such as the conduct of humanitarian operations as an example). Instead, "the social world is essentially relativistic and can only be understood from the point of view of the individuals who are directly involved in the activities which are to be studied." Hence, "one can only 'understand' by occupying the frame of reference of the participant in the action."[46] To anti-positivists, there can be no such thing as an objective understanding of a subject of study. Understanding is instead inherently subjective.

Anti-positivism has an intellectual lineage dating to late 19th century thinkers including Max Weber and Wilhelm Dilthey. Unlike positivists, who assert that the same methodology can be applied in the natural and the social sciences, Weber, Dilthey, and subsequent anti-positivists have argued that the social sciences and humanities differ from the natural sciences and therefore require a different methodology. The key reason for this difference is that, contrary to the behavior of objects in nature, human interaction is subject to subjective influences such as human will, thought, and emotion. These influences cannot by their nature be observed objectively and for that matter cannot be accurately quantified.[47]

Paparone's typology is worth revisiting at this juncture as it is once again one of the few available sources that explicitly addresses this epistemological approach as it has been applied within doctrine. A word of caution is first necessary, however, since Paparone used the term "post-positivism," which in the case of his discussion may actually be a misnomer. Positivism, anti-positivism, and post-positivism are three different branches of epistemology altogether. Founded in the writings of Karl Popper, post-positivism differs from positivism as it rejects the existence of "truth." It does not, however, dispute either the existence of objective judgment or the existence of a neural perspective in relation to subject matter under assessment, which is where anti-positivism's key dispute with positivism lies.[48] The definition of post-positivism that Paparone gave in his typology seems to incorporate some aspects of both post-and anti-positivism, and attempts to un-muddle this are hampered by a lack of references to his source material.[49] Discussion below therefore proceeds cautiously but nevertheless uses Paparone's own terminology.

Paparone offered a brief analysis of the 2008 edition of FM 3-0 and of a Training and Doctrine Command (TRADOC) paper discussing design thinking that was published in the same year. The issue with nomenclature notwithstanding, he concluded that aspects of the 2008 edition of FM 3-0 are "moderately postpositivist," a newly-emergent doctrinal category. Rather than describing it's subject matter categorically, as Paparone observed of positivist doctrine, moderately post-positivist doctrine "would call for viewing the world through overlapping continua... this type of doctrine requires improvisation, mentally agility [sic], and collaborative military practitioners."[50] As an example of an "overlapping continua," he cited the "spectrum of conflict" concept contained within FM 3-0.[51]

In his analysis of the TRADOC paper, which was not a doctrine manual but which would go on to influence doctrine, Paparone concluded that it is "highly postpositivist:"

> Meaning in this doctrine type (perhaps this should be better named the "anti-doctrine") is more contextual and fleeting because high complexity prohibits the ability to even imagine what is happening

or what will happen next. In this type, how we make sense is paradoxically "non-routine" where learning [is] ephemeral in a real-time dynamic.[52]

In other words, this type of doctrine acknowledges that ideas that may work right now are unlikely to work even a short time into the future and that no amount of planning will ever be able to accurately predict all possible consequences of any action taken. This type of doctrine is also difficult to apply due to a large number of interactive variables that must be taken into account and the prospects of military success are acknowledged as more open to the influence of chance, perception, and other subjective factors than they are in positivist doctrine. In essence, the advantage of this doctrine is that it allows those "inside" a situation to develop a greater understanding of the situation itself and of a greater proportion of the possible impacts of their actions.[53] Although not directly mentioned by Paparone, doctrinal discussions of "design" fit into this doctrinal category, which (as elaborated above) is arguably more anti- than post-positivist owing to its inherent subjectivity.

Debating Design: What the Proponents and Detractors Think

Unsurprisingly in a large organization such as the military, the introduction of anti-positivist approaches into doctrine has not been without debate. Proponents of design and other concepts applying anti-positivist approaches have lauded their employment of non-linear thinking, problem framing and emphasis on the role of subjective factors such as culture, environment, interconnectedness, and adaptation.[54] Several papers by US military practitioners (particularly Army officers) have analyzed these concepts and offered interpretations, supporting concepts or guidance to assist with their application.[55] Paparone (in addition to the typology discussed above) wrote a seven-part series of articles for *Small Wars Journal* which analyzed the applicability of design thinking to various areas of military endeavor including leadership, ethics, and planning.[56]

Those who detract from these approaches fall into one of two camps, with those in the first camp being opposed to the concepts themselves. William F. Owen, for example, dismisses many of the terms used in systems thinking as "good old wine in shabby new bottles," arguing that the new concepts (and their terminology in particular) confuses what was previously well understood anyway without adding any value to military operations.[57] Offering a more refined analysis of the theoretical framework underlying systems theory, Milan Vego warns that its application by the military is doomed to failure. In addition to critiquing the concept itself, he offers in support of his case an analysis of the IDF's problematic application of SOD during the 2006 conflict in Lebanon.[58]

In the second camp are those who feel that anti-positivist concepts are valid but that their application has gone, or perhaps inevitably will go, astray. The reasons underlying their concerns vary. Adam Elkus and Crispin Burke warn that although design is highly useful in framing operational and strategic problems, at the tactical level its vague language and acceptance of uncertainty may actually be counter-productive.[59] In a similar vein, Alex Vohr observes that design is geared towards counterinsurgency operations, where time allows for a detailed understanding of a situation to be developed. He questions its appropriateness to conventional operations concluding that in this type of warfare, "problem framing runs the risk of 'paralysis through analysis.'"[60] Greenwood and Hammes offer 10 criticisms of design thinking as applied by the US Army. Key amongst these is their assertion that design includes some of the key aspects of problem framing but either omits, over-simplifies, or misinterprets several others, hence severely constraining its potential to be effectively applied. Furthermore, they express concern that military culture may ultimately result in design thinking being boiled down to just another checklist, which would encourage the exact opposite of what design thinking sets out to achieve.[61]

Between the US and other English speaking western militaries, Fleck's "thought collectives" (as identified by Coombs) appear to be functioning in the same manner as they have previously.[62] In Australia and Canada, ideas shaped by chaos theory and complexity science have been featured in both doctrine and concept papers.[63] Most recently, US design doctrine has been evaluated in military journals published in both countries leading one to hypothesize that it is only a matter of time before the concept appears in their doctrine manuals.[64] Although the British Armed Forces do not yet seem to have debated design, they have nevertheless incorporated other anti-positivist ideas into their own counterinsurgency doctrine.[65] They have also released a joint doctrine manual entitled *Understanding,* which they define as "the ability to place knowledge in its wider context to provide us with options for decision making."[66] The thought and analysis processes advanced by this manual are noteworthy because they occupy a similar position to design in relation to the military planning process. The manual also addresses an array of similar anti-positivist ideas including the impact of culture, judgment, and human nature on decision making.[67]

Despite this debate having served to highlight several areas where improvement is warranted, it can be concluded that a doctrinal experiment with anti-positivism has well and truly commenced. This indicates that the military belief system itself may be shifting substantially as a result of recent conflicts, particularly those in Iraq and Afghanistan. Even if this is not the case, at the very least the belief system is going through a period of openness to new ideas. The significance and implications of this possibility are addressed in the next chapter.

Notes

1. These manuals include: Headquarters, Department of the Army, FM 5-0 *The Operations Process,* Washington, DC: U.S. Government Printing Office, March 2010; Headquarters, U.S. Marine Corps, MCWP 5-1 *Marine Corps Planning Process,* Washington, DC: U.S. Government Printing Office, 24 August 2010; Joint Chiefs of Staff, U.S. Department of Defense, JP 5-0 *Joint Operation Planning,* Washington, DC: U.S. Government Printing Office, August 11, 2011.

2. Phil Johnson & Joanne Duberley, *Understanding Management Research: An Introduction to Epistemology,* London: Sage Publications, 2000, pp. 12-19, quote p. 19. The exact dates of the start and finish of the Enlightenment is the subject of ongoing debate. The earliest point at which the Enlightenment is identified as commencing is the publication of Isaac Newton's *Principia Mathematica* in 1687, and the latest point at which it is identified as a dominant intellectual paradigm is shortly after the onset of the French Revolutionary Wars. Margaret C. Jacob, *The Enlightenment: A Brief History with Documents,* Boston: Bedford/St Martins, 2001, pp. 1-72.

3. This summary has been derived from the insight offered by Isaiah Berlin, as quoted in: Johnson & Duberley, *Understanding Management Research,* p. 13. Gendered language has been intentionally employed in this description as it reflects the highly-gendered nature of the intellectual discourse of the Enlightenment. It should also be observed that the intellectual discourse of the Enlightenment was shaped by discoveries in the mechanistic scientific regime identified by Bousquet. Indeed, the perception of the world as several component parts subject to a single set of overarching laws is metaphorically similar to the functioning of a clockwork mechanism. See: Antoine Bousquet, *The Scientific Way of Warfare: Order and Chaos on the Battlefields of Modernity,* London: Hurst & Co., 2009, pp. 38-50.

4. Johnson & Duberley, *Understanding Management Research,* pp. 13-14.

5. For a discussion of the influences on Comte's own intellectual development, as well as an overview of the impact of his writings, see: Gertrud Lenzer, ed., *Auguste Comte and Positivism: The Essential Writings,* New York, NY: Harper & Row, 1975, pp. xvii-lxviii.

6. For a discussion of these writers, see: Johnson & Duberley, *Understanding Management Research,* pp. 21-27.

7. Auguste Comte, "Plan of the Scientific Operations Necessary for Reorganizing Society" [1822]. Reproduced in: Lenzer, ed., *Auguste Comte and Positivism,* pp. 57-61.

8. Christopher R. Paparone, "FM 3-0: Operations on the Cusp of Post-positivism," *Small Wars Journal,* May 2008, available from *http://smallwars-journal.com/blog/journal/docs-temp/65-paparone.pdf,* accessed on February 17, 2011.

9. Additional results of Paparone's analysis are discussed in the next section of this chapter.

10. Paparone, "FM 3-0: Operations on the Cusp of Post-positivism."

11. Paparone, "FM 3-0: Operations on the Cusp of Post-positivism."

12. Paparone, "FM 3-0: Operations on the Cusp of Post-positivism."

13. Paparone, "FM 3-0: Operations on the Cusp of Post-positivism."

14. This assertion is based on the author's observations of themes present across scores of doctrine manuals produced by a half dozen or so English-speaking militaries, as well as translations of a few significant manuals produced by European militaries and many secondary source analyses of even more. Listing all of these doctrine manuals and related sources here would result in an unmanageably long endnote, so no attempt will be made to do so. Readers interested in more information about which manuals were consulted in making this assessment should note that all of the doctrine manuals referred to in the second and third chapters contain examples of positivist approaches to their subject matter. Furthermore, manuals in the second and third schools are more strongly and uniformly positivist than those in the fourth. Readers interested in further information about how they can access doctrine manuals are encouraged to consult: Bert Chapman, *Military Doctrine: A Reference Handbook*, Santa Barbara, CA: Praeger Security International, 2009.

14. There is a slight discrepancy in the wording of the U.S. and NATO definitions, but this is not substantial enough to impact on the underlying meaning, which is the same in both cases. Joint Chiefs of Staff, U.S. Department of Defense, JP 1-02, *Department of Defense Dictionary of Military and Associated Terms*, as amended through August 2009, p. 171; NATO, *NATO-Russia Glossary of Contemporary Political and Military Terms*, Brussels: NATO-Russia Joint Editorial Working Group, undated by promulgated online on June 8, 2001, p. 77, available from *www.nato.int/docu/glossary/eng/index.htm*, accessed on December 20, 2008.

16. The temporal relationship between the observer and subject is also observed by Paparone, who determines that highly-positivist doctrine is "present-to-past" oriented, while moderately positivist doctrine is "present-to-future" oriented. Unfortunately, he does not provide a great deal of detail about his reasoning in reaching this conclusion. Paparone, "FM 3-0: Operations on the Cusp of Postpositivism."

17. For an overview of these trends, see: Azar Gat, *A History of Military Thought: From the Enlightenment to the Cold War*, Oxford: Oxford University Press, 2001, Bk I, Pt 2, Bk II & Bk III. A more cynical observer might be forgiven for thinking that the caveat has been included as a disclaimer, in case the application of doctrine goes awry.

18. This criticism emerged within military circles about forty years after critiques of positivism had become widespread within the academic community

during the 1960s. Johnson & Duberley, *Understanding Management Research*, pp. 27-36.

19. Stephen R. Mann, "Chaos Theory and Strategic Thought," *Parameters*, Vol. XXII, Autumn 1992, pp. 56-57.

20. These critiques include: Mann, "Chaos Theory and Strategic Thought," pp. 54-68; Gary R. Schamburg, *Cloud Patterns: An Operational Hierarchy?* Unpublished monograph, Fort Leavenworth, KS: School of Advanced Military Studies, Academic Year 1994-5; H. R. McMaster, "On War: Lessons to be Learned," *Survival*, Vol. 50, No. 1, February-March 2008, pp. 19-30; Matthew Lauder, "Systemic Operational Design: Freeing Operational Planning from the Shackles of Linearity," *Canadian Military Journal*, Vol. 9, No. 4, 2009, pp. 41-49; Paparone, "FM 3-0: Operations on the Cusp of Postpositivism"; Christopher R. Paparone, "Design and the Prospects for Decision," *Small Wars Journal*, November 2010, available online from *http://smallwarsjournal.com/blog/journal/docs-temp/598-paparone.pdf*, accessed October 2, 2012.

21. Some of John Boyd's theories provide an early example of the application of chaos and complexity theory to military thinking; Mann's "Chaos Theory and Strategic Thought" provides an early example of the application of chaos theory. For an early example of a book-length treatment of chaos theory, written during the mid-1990s and intended as an introductory guide for an audience of military practitioners, see: Glenn E. James, *Chaos Theory: The Essentials for Military Applications*, Newport Paper No. 10, Newport, RI: Naval War College, 1996. On the relationship between Boyd and chaos and complexity theory, see: Frans P. B. Osinga, *Science, Strategy and War: The Strategic Theory of John Boyd, London: Rutledge, 2007, pp. 52-127.* Mann, "Chaos Theory and Strategic Thought," p. 57.

22. Michael Evans, "From Kadesh to Kandahar: Military Theory and the Future of War," *Naval War College Review*, Vol. LVI, No. 3, Summer 2003, p. 135.

23. Lieutenant General Paul K. Van Riper, quoted in Christopher Bassford, "Doctrinal Complexity: Nonlinearity in Marine Corps Doctrine," in F. G. Hoffman & Gary Horne, eds., *Maneuver Warfare Science 1998,* Washington DC: Department of the Navy, U.S. Marine Corps, 1998, p. 9.

24. Bassford, "Doctrinal Complexity," pp. 10-11; Adam Elkus, "Complexity, Design, and Modern Operational Art: U.S. Evolution or False Start?" *Canadian Army Journal*, Vol. 13, No. 3, Autumn 2010, pp. 57-58.

26. Bassford, "Doctrinal Complexity", p. 11.

27. See for example: Thomas E. Ricks, *The Gamble: General Petraeus and the Untold Story of the American Surge in Iraq, 2006-2008,* New York: Allen Lane, 2009, esp. pp. 24-31.

28. The process of its development, although touted by some as unique due to the scope of its consultation both inside and outside of the military, was

actually akin to the a mixture of the development process for third and fourth school doctrine manuals. The scale of the consultation was similar to that which occurred during the development of the 1982 edition of FM 100-5. On the development of FM 3-24, see: See: Ricks, *The Gamble*, pp. 24-31; John Nagl, "The Evolution and Importance of Army/Marine Corps Field Manual 3-24, Counterinsurgency," *Small Wars Journal* Blog Post, June 27, 2007, available from *http:// smallwarsjournal.com/blog/the-evolution-and-importance-of-armymarine-corps-field-manual-3-24-counterinsurgency*, accessed on April 5, 2012.

29. Philipp Rotmann, David Tohn & Jaron Wharton, "Learning Under Fire: Progress and Dissent in the U.S. Military," *Survival*, Vol. 54, No. 1, August-September 2009, pp. 38-41.

30. The most prominent example is a 2007 article by Lieutenant Colonel Paul Yingling, which asserted that "America's generals have failed to prepare our armed forces for war" in Iraq. In making his case, he argued that U.S. Army generals "miscalculated both the means and ways necessary to succeed in Iraq," that they "failed to adapt to the demands of counterinsurgency" and that "while the physical courage of America's generals is not in doubt, there is less certainty regarding their moral courage." Perhaps most famously, he stated that "a private who loses a rifle suffers far greater consequences than a general who loses a war." Paul Yingling, "A Failure in Generalship," *Armed Forces Journal*, May 2007, available from *www.armedforcesjournal.com/2007/05/2635198*, accessed on October 28, 2009.

31. Rotmann, Tohn & Wharton, "Learning Under Fire," p. 41; Martin L. Cook, "Revolt of the Generals: A Case Study in Professional Ethics," *Parameters*, Vol. XXXVIII, No. 1, pp. 4-15.

32. Rotmann, Tohn & Wharton, "Learning Under Fire," pp. 31-48.

33. Most notably these civilians included David Kilcullen, Conrad Crane and Emma Sky, amongst many others.

34. Ricks, *The Gamble*, pp. 20-21.

35. Walter E. Kretchik, *U.S. Army Doctrine: From the American Revolution to the War on Terror*, Lawrence, KS: University Press of Kansas, 2011, pp. 260-264.

36. Nagl, "The Evolution and Importance of Army/Marine Corps Field Manual 3-24, Counterinsurgency."

37. Headquarters, Department of the Army & Headquarters, U.S. Marine Corps, FM 3-24/MCWP 3-33.5 *Counterinsurgency,* Washington, DC: U.S. Government Printing Office, December 15, 2006, chap. 3. This reference (along with all subsequent references made herein) is to the content of the U.S. Army/USMC edition of the manual, not to the subsequent Chicago University Press edition.

38. Bousquet, *The Scientific Way of Warfare*, pp. 163-184.

39. Headquarters, Department of the Army & Headquarters, U.S. Marine Corps, FM 3-24/MCWP 3-33.5, paras. 4.2-4.3.

40. Nagl, "The Evolution and Importance of Army/Marine Corps Field Manual 3-24, Counterinsurgency."

41. William T. Sorrels, Glen R. Downing, Paul J. Blakesley, David W. Pendall, Jason K. Walk & Richard D. Wallwork, *Systemic Operational Design: An Introduction,* unpublished monograph: School of Advanced Military Studies, U.S. Army Command and General Staff College, academic year 2004-5, pp. 7-13, available from *www.dtic.mil/cgi-bin/GetTRDoc?AD=ADA479311*, accessed on April 11, 2012.

42. Kretchik, *U.S. Army Doctrine*, pp. 269-77.

43. Headquarters, Department of the Army, FM 5-0 *The Operations Process,* Washington, DC: U.S. Government Printing Office, March 2010, chap. 3.

44. Headquarters, U.S. Marine Corps, MCWP 5-1 *Marine Corps Planning Process,* Washington, DC: U.S. Government Printing Office, 24 August 2010, chap. 2. A draft version of this new manual was released in August 2009. For a critique of the draft manual, see: Jonathan M. Stofka, *Designing the Desired State: A Process and Model for Operational Design,* unpublished Masters thesis: Marine Corps University Command and Staff College, academic year 2009-10, available from *www.mcu.usmc.mil/Student%20Research/STOFKA%20-%20 MMS%20Paper%20AY%202010.pdf*, accessed on April 10, 2012.

45. Joint Chiefs of Staff, U.S. Department of Defense, JP 5-0 *Joint Operation Planning,* Washington, DC: U.S. Government Printing Office, August 11, 2011, chap. 3.

46. Gibson Burrell & Gareth Morgan, *Sociological Paradigms and Organisational Analysis: Elements of the Sociology of Corporate Life*, Portsmouth: Heinemenn, 1979, p. 5.

47. David Goddard, "Max Weber and the Objectivity of Social Science," *History and Theory*, Vol. 12, No. 1, 1973, pp. 1-22; Rudolf Makkreel, "Wilhelm Dilthey," in Edward N. Zalta, ed., *The Stanford Encyclopedia of Philosophy,* Summer 2012 edition, forthcoming. Available from *http://plato.stanford.edu/ archives/sum2012/entries/dilthey/*, accessed on April 13, 2012.

48. For post-positivism, there is no such thing as "truth" because nothing can ever be proven "true" beyond any doubt, no matter how small this doubt may be. Even in instances where there is absolutely no doubt now, it cannot ever be guaranteed that doubt will not appear sometime in the future. There is, however, such a thing as "false," and valid knowledge is derived by the rejection of things that can be proven false and the retention of things that have

not yet been (or cannot yet be) proven false. The means of determining that something is false can, however, be objective in nature. Johnson & Duberley, *Understanding Management Research*, pp. 27-33.

49. Paparone's definition of post-positivism, given here verbatim, is: "Postpositivism is nested in the worldview that humans always are biased in their 'objective' perceptions of reality; hence, this orientation permits going beyond an empirical sense of reality (i.e. we can **never** be positive about the way the world of military operations works). Postpositivism suggest that we can only approach the truth of reality, but can never really explain it fully; hence, to appreciate the complexity of life we humans must learn to value **multiple perspectives**. There can be no one best way of examining the complicated truth; hence, **interdisciplinary** interpretations are necessary to study reality. Rather than pursuing a quest for an objective, physical sense of reality, postpositivism demands we have to **make** sense of it all (and accept that this sensemaking is **subject** to change). Postpositivism does not reject positivism outright, but subordinates the view" [original emphasis]. Paparone, "FM 3-0: Operations on the Cusp of Postpositivism."

50. Paparone, "FM 3-0: Operations on the Cusp of Post-positivism.

51. This concept is located at: Headquarters, Department of the Army, FM 3-0 *Operations,* Washington DC: U.S. Government Printing Office, February 22, 2008, chap. 2.

52. Paparone, "FM 3-0: Operations on the Cusp of Post-positivism.

53. 53. Paparone, "FM 3-0: Operations on the Cusp of Post-positivism."

54. For example, see: Edward C. Cardon & Steve Leonard, "Unleashing Design: Planning and the Art of Battle Command," *Military Review*, Vol. 90, No. 2, March/April 2010, pp. 2-12; Huba Wass de Czege, "Systemic Operational Design: Learning and Adapting in Complex Missions," *Military Review*, Vol. 89, No. 1, January/February 2009, pp. 2-12; Ketti Davidson, "From Tactical Planning to Operational Design," *Military Review*, Vol. 88, No. 5, September/October 2008, pp. 33-39.

55. For example, see: Celestino Perez Jr., "A Practical Guide to Design: A Way to Think About It, and A Way to Do It," *Military Review*, Vol. 91, No. 2, March/April 2011, pp. 41-51; Xander Bullock & Bruce Vitor, "Design: How, Not Why," *Military Review*, Vol. 90. No. 2, March/April 2010, pp. 102-108; Stefan J. Banach & Alex Ryan, "The Art of Design: A Design Methodology," *Military Review*, Vol. 89, No. 2, March/April 2009, pp. 105-115.

56. For a list of articles in *Small Wars Journal* that have been authored or co-authored by Paparone, see: *http://smallwarsjournal.com/author/chris-paparone,* accessed on October 25, 2012.

57. William F. Owen, "Essay: The War of New Words: Why Military History Trumps Buzzwords," *Armed Forces Journal*, November 2009, available

from *www.armedforcesjournal.com/2009/11/4114043*, accessed on April 17, 2012.

58. Milan N. Vego, "A Case Against Systemic Operational Design," Joint Force Quarterly, No. 53, 2nd Quarter 2009, pp. 69-75.

59. Adam Elkus, & Crispin Burke, "Operational Design: Promise and Problems," *Small Wars Journal*, February 2010, pp. 16-17. Available from *http://smallwarsjournal.com/blog/journal/docs-temp/362-elkus.pdf*, accessed on April 16, 2012.

60. J. Alex Vohr, "Design in the Context of Operational Art," *Marine Corps Gazette*, Vol. 94, No. 1, January 2010, pp. 39-42.

61. T. C. Greenwood & T. X. Hammes, "War Planning for Wicked Problems: Where Joint Doctrine Fails," *Armed Forces Journal*, December 2009, available from *www.armedforcesjournal.com/2009/12/4252237*, accessed on April 16, 2012.

62. Howard G. Coombs, "In the Wake of a Paradigm Shift: The Canadian Forces College and the Operational Level of War (1987-1995)," *Canadian Military Journal*, Vol. 10, No. 2, 2010, pp. 19-27. For a critique of design doctrine from a German perspective (published in English), which implicitly suggests that a military thought collective exists between the U.S. and each of its NATO allies, see: Christof Schaefer, "Design: Extending Military Relevance," *Military Review*, Vol. 89, No. 5, September/October 2009, pp. 29-39.

63. For a summary of these developments, including an account of an anomalous if temporary situation in which the Canadian and Australian armies embraced the idea of operational complexity without the usual reference to their larger allies, see: Aaron P. Jackson, "Moving Beyond Manoeuvre: A Conceptual Coming-of-age for the Australian and Canadian Armies," *Australian Defence Force Journal*, No. 177, November/December 2008, pp. 85-100. See also: Australian Army, *Adaptive Campaigning: The Land Force Response to Complex Warfighting,* Version 4.18, reproduced as Appendix 2 to Scott Hopkins, ed., *Chief of Army's Exercise Proceedings 2006,* Duntroon: Australian Army Land Warfare Studies Centre, 2006, pp. 143–171; Andrew B. Godefroy, ed., *Land Operations 2021: Adaptive Dispersed Operations—A Force Employment Concept for Canada's Army of Tomorrow,* Kingston, ON: Directorate of Land Concepts and Doctrine, 2007.

64. For example, see: Lauder, "Systemic Operational Design," pp. 41-49; David L. Walker, "Refining the Military Appreciation Process for Adaptive Campaigning," *Australian Army Journal*, Vol. 8, No. 2, Winter 2011, pp. 85-100.

65. These included reprinting the "paradoxes of counterinsurgency" section of the U.S. Army's FM 3-24; instructions on "developing a narrative"; and a discussion of the role of conundrum. British Army, Field Manual Volume 1 Part 10, *Countering Insurgency*, Army Code 71876, Warminster: Land Warfare Centre, October 2009.

66. UK Ministry of Defence, Joint Doctrine Publication (JDP) 04 *Understanding,* Shrivenham, UK: Development Concepts and Doctrine Centre, December 2010, p. iii.

67. UK Ministry of Defence, JDP 04 *Understanding,* esp. chaps. 3-4.

Chapter 5

Significance and Implications

The nature, scope, and content of doctrine can only be fully understood in light of the intellectual context in which it is written. In addition to well-known influences such as military operations and national strategies, other lesser realized influences that shape this intellectual context include culture, both national and service; intellectual trends in the natural and social sciences, and in the humanities; the relationships between military institutions, states and societies; and a host of other factors.

Previous chapters have shed light on these influences through an analysis of the ontology and epistemology of military doctrine. This chapter builds on this analysis to address the significance and implications for contemporary military doctrine, strategy, and operations. Discussion proceeds in four sections, with the first asserting that a significant "paradigm shift" is currently underway regarding what constitutes an acceptable military belief system. The second section discusses possible directions in which military strategic and conceptual thinking may evolve in the near future. The third section discusses implications for the relationships between militaries and other agencies. In the fourth section, discussion turns to the benefits ontology and epistemology potentially yield for conceptual and terminological clarity.

Paradigm Shifts

As defined herein, doctrine is the most visible representation of a military's institutional belief system. This belief system regards the accepted paradigms by which a military understands, prepares for and (at least in theory) conducts warfare. These paradigms are themselves corollaries of the perceptions a military has of its institutional role and legitimacy within broader society, hence these aspects of a military's belief system are also discernible through its doctrine, albeit at a greater level of abstraction. For this reason, doctrine constitutes an institutional discourse which is reflective of the dominant modes of military thinking during various epochs. Historical analysis, such as that conducted in previous chapters, offers insights into to how this belief system has changed over time.

From the analysis above, it can be seen that the nature of this discourse has undergone several of what Thomas Kuhn identified as "paradigm shifts." A "paradigm," as defined by Kuhn, exists amongst a community of scientific practitioners who base their research upon a "coherent tradition," which encompasses "law, theory, application and instrumentation together"[1]—what might otherwise be understood as a shared belief system.[2] This coherent tradition provides a common set of rules and establishes accepted standards that form the basis for further research within the paradigm. From time-to-time, the coherent tradition is challenged, causing a "paradigm in crisis" followed eventually by a "revolution" that introduces a new paradigm and therefore establishes a new tradition.[3]

For doctrine, each of the four "schools of doctrinal ontology" identified above constitutes one such paradigm. The concepts and theories developed within the doctrine manuals constituting each school are analogous to the research undertaken within each of Kuhn's communities of scientific practitioners with the different scope of each school representing the coherent tradition underlying this research. In line with Kuhn's hypothesis, these traditions have undergone periods of "crisis," leading to the emergence of a new school of doctrinal ontology and therefore establishing a new tradition.

There is, however, one important departure from Kuhn's thesis. Kuhn determines that the emergence of a new paradigm will lead to the previous paradigm gradually disappearing. While this is true of certain concepts and theories that have appeared in doctrine, risen in favor to a pinnacle and then fallen out of favor and disappeared, it is not true of the schools themselves. Rather, each of the different schools of doctrinal ontology have continued to exist alongside one another, in this respect being more akin to the scientific "regimes" identified by Bousquet.[4] Equating a regime to a "social paradigm," Bousquet defers to Fritjof Capra, who defines it as "a constellation of concepts, values, perceptions, and practices shared by a community which forms a particular vision of reality that is the basis of the way the community organizes itself."[5] For Bousquet, the appearance and rise to dominance of one regime does not eliminate another but rather the two regimes come to exist alongside each other and may even be complimentary. This has certainly been the case with doctrine where paradigm shifts have exposed the limits of previous paradigms but have not rendered them either useless or antiquated.

Significantly, a paradigm shift appears currently to be underway. Furthermore, this shift is arguably the most pervasive to have occurred in 400 years of doctrinal history. The reason for this is that it is an epistemological rather than an ontological shift. The emergence in recent years of concepts grounded in anti-positivism, in particular those related to chaos theory and the complexity sciences, are challenging existing doctrinal paradigms at a more fundamental level. These new concepts question longstanding assumptions made within all four schools of doctrinal ontology, for example by proposing that knowledge acquisition is subjective rather than objective, and by readily accepting and working within, rather than attempting to regulate around, remove, or simply ignore, the existence of metaphysical factors such as culture, chance, and human will.

This paradigm shift is far from complete, however. According to Kuhn, "during the transition period there will be a large but never complete overlap between the problems that can be solved by the old and new paradigm but there will also be a decisive difference in the modes of solution."[6] The existence at present of such a state of affairs is clear from the nature of doctrine manuals that incorporate anti-positivist approaches. As Elkus observed, these concepts are still the doctrinal equivalent of a "first draft" and numerous criticisms such as those summarized in chapter 4 will need to be addressed before the paradigm shift can be declared complete.[7]

There is also the possibility that the incorporation of anti-positivist approaches into doctrine may turn out to be a flirtation rather than an actual paradigm shift. This possibility may come to fruition for any number of reasons. Perhaps, as Greenwood and Hammes observe, it may simply be beyond the institutional capacity of military organizations to accept such a fundamental variation to their world view.[8] Alternatively, hitherto low-key critiques of Israel's performance during the 2006 war in Lebanon may be yet to have their full impact on the US discourse and may ultimately serve to undermine the approach itself.[9] In the US case, most anti-positivist doctrine came about as a result of its own wars in Iraq and Afghanistan. As these wars come to an end, another possibility is that doctrine writers may move away from them in favor of a return to more traditional approaches.[10]

A fourth potential reason is the changing nature of strategic challenges. As Elkus and Bourke contend:

> ...the complexity experienced in the context of new wars is mostly complexity generated by specifically American factors— grand strategic uncertainty, the growing doctrinal problem of "compression" and its relationship to a dysfunctional "whole of government" approach and geopolitical shifts in American strategic primacy.[11]

The implication of this contention is that should American grand strategy enter a period of renewed certainty, anti-positivism may well disappear from doctrine. The incorporation of design thinking into the 2011 edition of Joint Publication (JP) 5-0 *Joint Operation Planning* notwithstanding, anti-positivist doctrine in the US military has thus far been limited to the Army and Marine Corps. As the US strategic focus shifts towards the Asia-Pacific,[12] the Navy and Air Force have recently developed an "AirSea Battle" concept for use in this theatre. This concept sits very comfortably within the third school of doctrinal ontology (even its name is immediately reminiscent of the main operating concept contained in the 1982 edition of Field Manual (FM) 100-5 *Operations*) and its underlying epistemology is unquestionably positivist.[13]

Despite this array of possibilities, historical precedence suggests that the new doctrinal paradigm will most likely solidify and eventually take its place alongside previous paradigms. Already the debate summarized in the previous chapter indicates that several of the issues yet to be resolved are under discussion in scholarly and military forums. Again historical precedence indicates that the result of these debates is likely to shape doctrine over the coming years and indeed, the state of the non-doctrinal debate is already yielding clues as to how anti-positivist doctrine may evolve in the next few years.

Possible Avenues for Doctrinal Evolution

By evaluating both the state of the debate about anti-positivist concepts and the evolution anti-positivism within existing doctrine, one can deduce several issues that still need to be addressed. Despite the difficulties that satisfactorily resolving these issues pose, addressing them will nevertheless be necessary before a paradigm shift can be said to have completely occurred.

One of the issues that will need to be addressed concerns the appropriateness of the extent of anti-positivist doctrine. It has already been acknowledged that anti-positivist approaches are more applicable at the strategic and operational levels than at the tactical,[14] however this debate may yet go a step further. In an influential monograph, Justin Kelly and Mike Brennan recently posited that "operational art" has now expanded to the extent that it has "devoured" several aspects of strategy. They call for operational art to re-focus on bridging tactical encounters and for a reassertion of strategy to fill all of the other areas currently absorbed by operational art.[15] This has triggered renewed debate as to what the role and extent of the operational level of war and its relationship to tactics and strategy should be. It is possible that a reconsideration of this construct taking into account alternate epistemological approaches will emerge, leading tactics and (a constrained re-definition of) operations to be assigned to the realms of positivist doctrine and a reasserted strategic level to be assigned to that of anti-positivism.

A second issue concerns the means of translating understanding derived through anti-positivist approaches into practical results and to date, this area remains underdeveloped. Given that anti-positivism emphasizes subjectivity, it challenges the legitimacy of most if not all traditional mechanisms for measuring the results of military operations. In place of this, anti-positivism stresses the importance of **perception**: victory or defeat exists only as it is perceived by participants in conflict (be they friendly, enemy, civilians, or neutral fourth-party observers). Furthermore, these perceptions are likely to change over time and are unlikely to be "black and white." How to work within this conceptual framework and where victory can never be considered as either "complete" or "total," remains an issue to be resolved.[16]

Thirdly, the clarity of the nomenclature needs to be addressed. As things stand, several terms that imply anti-positivist approaches are routinely misapplied within positivist constructs. Perhaps the most common example of this is the tendency over the past decade or so for seemly every military problem to be labeled as "complex," usually without any attempt to determine what this actually means or what its ramifications may be.[17] This problem is the manifestation of the latest terminological fad, wherein the language of an emerging idea has been adopted without the doctrine writer being fully aware of, understanding or appreciating the idea itself. The same could be said for several other terms associated with anti-positivism, including (but certainly not limited to) "knowledge," "understanding," "adaptation," and even "design," which should more correctly be referred to as "design thinking."[18] Beyond doctrine, this is also a common problem within strategic policy and concepts.

Finally, there are two prominent "gaps" that need to be filled. First, there exists at present a "comprehension gap:" despite having developed an awareness of anti-positivist concepts such as design, many strategists and military practitioners are not yet aware of the epistemological roots of these concepts or of the implications of these roots. Second, there exists also an "application gap," the bolting of anti-positivist ideas onto existing positivist ones has caused this. Both of these problems are epitomized by the current placing of design at the beginning of existing operational planning processes. A detailed assessment of the nature of anti-positivist concepts that takes explicitly into account their epistemology may yet determine that their application at the strategic or operational level requires a separate planning process than the application of other doctrine at the operational or tactical level and that a bridging construct is necessary between the two. In short, the further development of the new epistemological approach is likely to have a greater impact on doctrinal ontology than has yet been forthcoming.

Understanding Relationships

Another implication of the analysis herein concerns the ill-explored nature of the relationships between militaries and other actors. In the past few decades, there has been a growing discussion of the need for strategic and operational approaches that are "whole of government," "interagency," "multinational," or some other term implying cooperation between militaries and other organizations.[19] The employment of these terms indicates an increased awareness of the nexus of relationships that exist between militaries and other parties. The (in)famous "dynamic planning for counterinsurgency in Afghanistan" diagram perhaps constitutes the most extreme manifestation of this awareness.[20] Yet for all the criticism this diagram has attracted, it is nevertheless an excellent example of the application of chaos theory and complexity science in attempting to solve a military problem.[21]

Anti-positivist approaches offer a new mechanism for understanding relationships between, and for that matter within, militaries. As observed above, the impact of service culture upon military conduct remains seldom-explored,[22] as does the relationship between the militaries of different states.[23] Both of these areas require further exploration especially in light of the emerging American strategic refocus on the Asia-Pacific region. Tentative steps have recently been taken towards a comprehensive reassessment of western (read English speaking in this instance) understanding of non- western military culture, history, and ideas.[24] The application of alternative epistemological approaches, most notably those associated with chaos theory and complexity science, yields substantial potential for the conduct of a more significant reassessment of the nature of the military challenges in this region. Increased cross-cultural understanding may, in turn, yield other potential sources to be tapped during future doctrine, concept, or even strategy development.

Closer to home, there has been another interesting development within the last decade. This monograph chronicles the expansion of

written doctrine **within** western militaries over the course of 400 years. Within the last few years, military-style doctrine—specifically that which could be assessed as fitting within the fourth ontological school—has been released by other organizations. These include the United Nations and non-profit organizations, the latter of which have collaborated with the US military.[25] These manuals have been labeled "doctrine" by their sponsor organizations and have been developed specifically to mimic their military equivalents. While the dissemination of ideas and concepts between militaries on one hand and non-government organizations, the business world, and academia on the other is not new, the creation of military-style doctrine by other organizations is. This attests to the legitimacy with which doctrine is now viewed as a mechanism for transmitting an institutional discourse. It also signifies that other organizations appreciate the appeal of doctrine to the military audience. The implication of this for enhanced interoperability cannot be overstated but due to the recentness of this development it is still too early to determine what its ultimate impact will be.

Conceptual and Terminological Clarity

Another significant implication of discussion herein is the realization that most of the factors that have affected doctrine development have, for most of the existence of doctrine, done so subconsciously. For English speaking militaries, it was not until the 1980s that they explicitly defined their institutional ontology. Explicit discussion of military ontology and epistemology to date remains limited to a dozen papers or so. Yet awareness of these is of the utmost importance because:

> how we come to ask particular questions, how we assess the relevance and value of different research methodologies so that we can investigate those questions, how we evaluate the outputs of research, all express and vary according to our underlying epistemological commitments. Even though they often remain unrecognized by the individual, such epistemological commitments are a key feature of our pre-understandings which influence how we make things intelligible.[26]

At the opening of this monograph, it was observed that contemporary militaries are suffering from a glut of buzzwords and imprecise or ill-defined terms, ideas, and concepts. As a result, the number of terms and concepts that are vying for inclusion in doctrine are more numerous than ever before. An understanding of epistemology, and for that matter ontology, will give doctrine writers, strategists, statesmen, and military practitioners a hitherto untapped means by which to identify problems, propose solutions, and evaluate the worth of these proposals. Ultimately, this will lead to better doctrine and, if the rhetoric of the doctrine itself is to be believed, will in turn translate into more effective military practice.

Notes

1. Thomas S. Kuhn, *The Structure of Scientific Revolutions*, 3rd ed., Chicago, IL: Chicago University Press, 1996, pp. 10-11.

2. Howard G. Coombs, "In the Wake of a Paradigm Shift: The Canadian Forces College and the Operational Level of War (1987-1995)," *Canadian Forces Journal*, Vol. 10, No. 2, 2010, p. 20.

3. Kuhn, *The Structure of Scientific Revolutions*, pp. 10-22, 84-91.

4. Antoine Bousquet, *The Scientific Way of Warfare: Order and Chaos on the Battlefields of Modernity*, London: Hirst and Co., 2009, p. 4.

5. Fritjof Capra, *The Web of Life: A New Scientific Understanding of Living Systems,* New York, NY: Anchor Books, 1997, pp. 5-6, quote p. 6.

6. Kuhn, *The Structure of Scientific Revolutions*, p. 85.

7. Adam Elkus, "Complexity, Design, and Modern Operational Art: U.S. Evolution or False Start?," *Canadian Army Journal,* Vol. 13, No. 3, Autumn 2010, p. 55.

8. T. C. Greenwood & T. X. Hammes, "War Planning for Wicked Problems: Where Joint Doctrine Fails," *Armed Forces Journal*, December 2009, available from *www.armedforcesjournal.com/2009/12/4252237*, accessed on April 16, 2012.

9. For an example of a critique along these lines, see: Milan N. Vego, "A Case Against Systemic Operational Design," Joint Force Quarterly, No. 53, 2nd Quarter 2009, pp. 69-75.

10. The abandonment of counterinsurgency theory within third and fourth school doctrine already appears to be underway, with future editions of the US Army's counterinsurgency doctrine manual likely to be relegated to the second school. Crucially for anti-positivist doctrine, however, this abandonment has not included design, which remains prominent within key doctrine manuals such as JP 5-0. Regarding the progress of what has been dubbed "the rise and fall of counterinsurgency," see: Fred Kaplan, "The End of the Age of Petraeus: The Rise and Fall of Counterinsurgency," *Foreign Affairs,* Vol. 92, No. 1 (January/ February 2013), pp. 75-90.

11. Adam Elkus & Crispin Burke, "Operational Design: Promise and Problems," *Small Wars Journal*, February 2010, p. 5, available from *http:// smallwarsjournal.com/blog/journal/docs-temp/362-elkus.pdf,* accessed on April 16, 2012.

12. U.S. Department of Defense, *Sustaining U.S. Global Leadership: Priorities for 21st Century Defense,* Washington, DC: U.S. Government Printing Office, January 2012, p. 2.

13. Andrew F. Krepinevich, *Why AirSea Battle?* Washington, DC: Centre for Strategic and Budgetary Assessments, 2010; Jan van Tol, with Mark

Gunzinger, Andrew F. Krepinevich & Jim Thomas, *AirSea Battle: A Point of Departure Operational Concept,* Washington, DC: Centre for Strategic and Budgetary Assessments, 2010.

14. Elkus & Burke, "Operational Design: Promise and Problems," pp. 16

15. Justin Kelly & Mike Brennan, *Alien: How Operational Art Devoured Strategy*, Carlisle, PA: U.S. Army Strategic Studies Institute, September 2009.

16. Although it does not employ an anti-positivist methodology, an excellent exploration of some of the issues surrounding the differences between perceptions and realities of "victory" is offered in: Ian Bickerton, *The Illusion of Victory: The True Costs of War,* Melbourne: Melbourne University Press, 2011.

17. Bousquet addresses this problem in far greater detail by means of conducting a comprehensive critique of the Network Centric Warfare concept. Bousquet, *The Scientific Way of Warfare*, pp. 215-33.

18. David L. Walker, "Refining the Military Appreciation Process for Adaptive Campaigning," *Australian Army Journal,* Vol. 8, No. 2, Winter 2011, pp. 96-98.

19. A decade earlier, the vogue term under discussion was "joint," the impetus then being to foster cooperation and collaboration between different services of a single military. This approach has arguably been so successful at the term "joint" is now generally accepted, and joint approaches to military endeavors are commonplace.

20. PA Consulting Group, *Dynamic Planning for Counterinsurgency in Afghanistan,* PowerPoint Presentation, dated 2009, available from *http:// msnbcme- dia.msn.com/i/MSNBC/Components/Photo/_new/Afghanistan_ Dynamic_Plan- ning.pdf*, accessed on May 1, 2012.

21. For an excellent short presentation on how to understand the utility of the diagram, see: Eric Berlow, *How Complexity Leads to Simplicity,* TED: Talks in Less Than Six Minutes, July 2010, available from *www.ted.com/talks/eric_ berlow_how_complexity_leads_to_simplicity.html*, accessed on May 15, 2012.

22. The few explorations undertaken to date include: Carl H. Builder *The Masks of War: American Military Styles in Strategy and Analysis,* Baltimore, MD: John Hopkins University Press, 1989; Allan D. English, *Understanding Military Culture: A Canadian Perspective,* Montreal, QC: McGill-Queens University Press, 2004.

23. Coombs' application of Fleck's "thought collectives" to Canada's adoption of the "levels of war" construct presents a rare example of an analysis of this relationship, albeit that his study is both geographically and temporally limited. Coombs, "In the Wake of a Paradigm Shift", pp. 19-27.

24. Most prominently, see: Patrick Porter, *Military Orientalism: Eastern War Through Western Eyes,* London: Hirst & Co, 2009.

25. United Nations (UN) Department of Peacekeeping Operations, *United Nations Peacekeeping Operations: Principles and Guidelines,* New York, NY: United Nations, January 18, 2008; United States Institute of Peace & U.S. Army Peacekeeping and Stability Operations Institute, *Guiding Principles for Stabilization and Reconstruction,* Washington, DC: United States Institute of Peace, 2009.

26. Phil Johnson & Joanne Duberley, *Understanding Management Research: An Introduction to Epistemology*, London: Sage Publications, 2000, p. 1.

Chapter 6

Conclusion

Defining military doctrine as expressive of a military's "belief system," this monograph has conducted an examination of the expansion and significance of its written form. This examination occurred first through an ontological and subsequently through an epistemological lens and links have been established between doctrine on one hand and professional military education, scientific discovery, the growth of the modern state, the increasing institutionalization and bureaucratization of society, and the evolution of thinking within philosophy and the social sciences on the other. From this examination, it is discernable that military doctrine is a product of its environment. It's a belief system that has been shaped, often subconsciously, by a diverse and seldom acknowledged array of factors.

The ontology of doctrine can be divided into four schools that can be labeled the technical manual, tactical manual, operational manual, and military strategic manual schools. The delineation of doctrinal ontology into these schools is based on three factors. First, the scope of the content and the intended audience broadens from one school to the next. Second, the manner in which manuals in each of these schools is applied varies, with the schools being respectively applied as instruction manuals, training aids, guidance and as an instrument for analysis.

Third, each manual has a different type of relationship to a military's accepted institutional ontology. Manuals in the first school do not engage with this ontology at all, focusing instead on describing micro- level processes in isolation from outside factors. Manuals in the second school offer only an implicit ontology. Those in the third offer an explicit ontology, which initially viewed militaries as subordinate to the state and as narrowly tasked with undertaking operations to defeat the (conventional) military forces of other states. Although recognition of the military's subordination to the state has remained central within this school, the range of military tasks envisioned has since expanded to include several other roles (including irregular warfare and a variety of operations other than war) and the various relationships militaries have with other organizations (both government and non-government) are now also addressed. Manuals in the fourth school are often used as a means to examine ontological questions, posing answers to these by way of establishing very general principles or a core conceptual framework for military activities.

The relationship between each of the schools is complicated and multi-faceted. It is also somewhat blurred and some manuals exhibit characteristics attributable to multiple schools. Despite this, the division of doctrine into four ontological schools is a useful mechanism for examining its evolution over time. When this evolution is examined from educational, scientific, and bureaucratic perspectives, the relationship between military doctrine, the institutional development of militaries themselves, and the changing nature of their relationship with society, is elucidated. Given that ontology examines the nature of being and the taxonomies used to define reality, it is unsurprising that the evolution of doctrine has been closely linked to these relationships.

Yet even as doctrine has evolved into each of the four schools, it has consistently been underpinned by ontological realism, a perspective that emphasizes that the world beyond human cognition is structured and tangible regardless of whether or not humans perceive and label it. The taxonomies propounded in doctrine have not been about defining and structuring reality. Rather, they have been about understanding reality and ultimately manipulating it, the intent being to achieve military victory as efficiently as possible. Where doctrine fails to sufficiently address a military's ontology or where the taxonomies that constitute that ontology are inappropriate, adherence to doctrine can potentially create a dissonance between tactical means and strategic ends, as doctrine becomes susceptible to providing ill-suited guidance when faced with situations outside of its remit.

Accompanying doctrine's ontological realism has been its positivist epistemology. This epistemology advocates a methodology wherein the subject of study (warfare) should be observed from a neutral viewpoint, with the results of the observation subsequently being assessed in a rational, objective manner. This allows the assessor to determine the universal laws governing relationships and, using this knowledge, to subsequently manipulate these relationships to achieve a desired end state (victory). By its nature this doctrine focuses on linear and therefore predictable cause- and-effect relationships. It is both logical and reductionist in its outlook. Its advantage is that it allows military practitioners to establish processes, both rigid (such as doctrine describing how to employ a weapons system) and flexible (such as doctrine detailing a military planning process). These processes are relatively easy to comprehend and follow, even in instances where departure from them may be encouraged in certain situations. The institutional belief system represented by this doctrine is one in which warranted knowledge is that which can be mathematically measured from an objective position.

Presently, doctrine may be (to paraphrase both Paparone and Kuhn) on the cusp of a paradigm shift.[1] This shift involves the emergence of doctrine based upon anti-positivist epistemology. Disputing the existence of objectivity altogether, anti-positivism emphasizes that everything is relative and that any attempt come to an understanding can only be undertaken from the perspective of a participant. All understanding is therefore inherently subjective and is affected by several intangible factors such as chance, perception, and human will. It is considered difficult if not impossible to accurately determine cause-and-effect relationships due to the concurrent interaction of multiple variables. Although more difficult to understand and apply, anti-positivist doctrine offers those who successfully do so the prospect of developing a greatly enhanced understanding of the situation they are facing and of the consequences of their actions, especially at the strategic and operational levels. "Design," featured in manuals such as the 2006 edition of Field Manual (FM) 3-24 *Counterinsurgency* and the 2011 edition of Joint Publication (JP) 5-0 *Joint Operation Planning*, is an example of the application of anti-positivism within doctrine.

It must be emphasized that the shift to anti-positivism is still embryonic, having commenced at most a few decades ago. The shift may therefore turn out to be a chimera, especially given the long-standing and entrenched nature of positivist military thinking and anti-positivism's relative difficulty to grasp. Indeed, current doctrine appears to graft anti- positivist concepts onto existing positivist ones, without deference to the epistemological confusion—and resultant conceptual perversion—that this causes. The conduct of a more detailed assessment of this new doctrinal paradigm from an epistemological perspective would be highly useful in determining whether to further develop or to abandon anti-positivist approaches. At best, their continued ad hoc application will translate into sub-optimal operational and, resultantly, strategic outcomes. Such an assessment may also assist as a mechanism for pruning existing concepts that either muddle these competing epistemological approaches or which use the language of one but the substance of another.

Ultimately, however, understanding the epistemology of military doctrine is important for far broader reasons. Doctrine, expressive of a military's institutional belief system, is a gauge for the way militaries view their role and therefore their institution, in relation to the states and societies that sustain them. The emergence of each new school of doctrinal ontology and more recently the inclusion of anti-positivist concepts within doctrine, indicate changes in a military's institutional understanding of its relationship with state and society. These changes have occurred for one of two reasons. First, formal (written) recognition of the military's role has replaced previously informal (verbal or implicit) recognition. Second, following the conclusion of the Cold War, changes in what states and societies expected of their militaries led these militaries to re-evaluate their role altogether.

This belief system also explains why a military may prefer a certain type of strategic approach and why it plans and conducts operations the way it does. The incorporation of anti-positivist approaches into doctrine has been partly due to the initial failure of positivist strategies and tactics during the wars of the early 21st century. The proliferation of new, anti-positivist doctrine, in particular the 2006 edition of FM 3-24, was accompanied by a change in overall strategy, which had a positive effect on the outcome of the war in Iraq in particular. This example illustrates the epistemological link between strategy and tactics on one hand and doctrine on the other.

The broad range of influences on military doctrine discussed in this monograph demonstrate that for most of its 400 year history, most of the factors that have influenced doctrine development have been at best implicitly understood and at worst not understood at all. The ontological and epistemological consideration of doctrine undertaken herein has helped to shed light on these influences. Since everyone adheres to a set of ontological and epistemological beliefs, whether they realize it or not, the advantage to military practitioners, strategists, statesmen, and doctrine writers of recognizing and understanding these beliefs is that better doctrine, better strategy, and ultimately better operational performance, will inevitably come of it.

Note

1. Christopher R. Paparone, "FM 3-0: Operations on the Cusp of Postpositivism," *Small Wars Journal*, May 2008, available from *http:// smallwarsjournal.com/blog/journal/docs/temp/65-paparone.pdf,* accessed on February 17, 2011; Thomas S. Kuhn, *The Structure of Scientific Revolutions,* 3rd ed., Chicago, IL: Chicago University Press, 1996, pp. 10-11.

Bibliography

Primary Sources

Doctrine Manuals

Australian Defence Force, Australian Defence Doctrine Publication Doctrine *Foundations of Australian Military Doctrine*, 1st ed., Canberra: Defence Publishing Service, May 2002.

Australian Defence Force, Australian Defence Doctrine Publication-Doctrine *Foundations of Australian Military Doctrine*, 2nd ed., Canberra: Defence Publishing Service, July 2005.

British Armed Forces, Joint Warfare Publication 0-01 *British Defence Doctrine*, 1st ed., London: Her Britannic Majesty's Stationary Office, 1997.

British Army, Field Manual Volume 1 Part 10, *Countering Insurgency*, Army Code 71876, Warminster: Land Warfare Centre, October 2009.

Canadian Forces, Canadian Forces Joint Publication 01 *Canadian Military Doctrine*, 1st ed., Ottawa, ON: Canadian Forces Experimentation Centre, April 2009, available from *www.cfd-cdf. forces.gc.ca/cfwc-cgfc/ Index/JD/Pub_Eng/Capstone/CFJP_%20 01_Canadian_Military_Doctrine_En_2009_04_Web.pdf*, accessed on March 4, 2011.

Canadian Forces, *Joint and Combined Operations,* Ottawa: Canadian National Defence Headquarters, 1995.

Directorate General Development and Doctrine, *Army Doctrine Publication: Land Operations,* United Kingdom: British Army, May 2005.

Headquarters, Department of the Army & Headquarters, U.S. Marine Corps, Field Manual 3-24/Marine Corps Warfighting Publication 3-33.5 *Counterinsurgency,* Washington, DC: U.S. Government Printing Office, December 15, 2006.

Headquarters, Department of the Army, Field Manual 1 *The Army,* Washington DC: U.S. Government Printing Office, June 14, 2001.

Headquarters, Department of the Army, Field Manual 1 *The Army,* Washington DC: U.S. Government Printing Office, June 2005.

Headquarters, Department of the Army, Field Manual 100-5 *Operations,* Washington DC: U.S. Government Printing Office, August 20, 1982.

Headquarters, Department of the Army, Field Manual 100-5 *Operations,* Washington DC: U.S. Government Printing Office, July 1, 1976.

Headquarters, Department of the Army, Field Manual 100-5 *Operations,* Washington DC: U.S. Government Printing Office, June 14, 1993.

Headquarters, Department of the Army, Field Manual 3-0 *Operations,* Washington DC: U.S. Government Printing Office, June 14, 2001.

Headquarters, Department of the Army, Field Manual 3-0 *Operations,* Washington DC: U.S. Government Printing Office, February 22, 2008.

Headquarters, Department of the Army, Field Manual 5-0 *The Operations Process,* Washington, DC: U.S. Government Printing Office, March 2010.

Headquarters, Department of the Navy, Navy Doctrine Publication 1 *Naval Warfare,* Washington, DC: U.S. Government Printing Office, March 28, 1994.

Headquarters, U.S. Air Force, Air Force Manual 1-1 (Volume 1), *Basic Aerospace Doctrine of the United States Air Force,* Washington, DC: U.S. Government Printing Office, March 1992.

Headquarters, U.S. Air Force, Air Force Manual 1-1 (Volume 2), *Basic Aerospace Doctrine of the United States Air Force,* Washington, DC: U.S. Government Printing Office, March 1992.

Headquarters, U.S. Marine Corps, Fleet Marine Force Manual 1 *Warfighting,* Washington, DC: U.S. Government Printing Office, March 6, 1989.

Headquarters, U.S. Marine Corps, Marine Corps Doctrine Publication 1 *Warfighting,* Washington DC: U.S. Government Printing Office, June 20, 1997.

Headquarters, U.S. Marine Corps, Marine Corps Doctrine Publication 1-1 *Strategy,* Washington DC: U.S. Government Printing Office, November 12, 1997.

Headquarters, U.S. Marine Corps, Marine Corps Doctrine Publication 1-2 *Campaigning,* Washington DC: U.S. Government Printing Office, August 1, 1997.

Headquarters, U.S. Marine Corps, Marine Corps Doctrine Publication

1-3 *Tactics,* Washington DC: U.S. Government Printing Office, July 30, 1997.

Headquarters, U.S. Marine Corps, Marine Corps Warfighting Publication 5-1 *Marine Corps Planning Process,* Washington, DC: U.S. Government Printing Office, 24 August 2010.

Joint Chiefs of Staff, U.S. Department of Defense, Joint Publication 1-02, *Department of Defense Dictionary of Military and Associated Terms,* as amended through August 2009.

Joint Chiefs of Staff, U.S. Department of Defense, Joint Publication 1 *Doctrine for the Armed Forces of the United States,* May 2, 2007, Incorporating Change 1, March 20, 2009, available from *www.dtic.mil/ doctrine/new_pubs/jp1.pdf,* accessed on March 4, 2011.

Joint Chiefs of Staff, U.S. Department of Defense, Joint Publication 1 *Joint Warfare of the Armed Forces of the United States*, Washington, DC: U.S. Government Printing Office, November 14, 2000.

Joint Chiefs of Staff, U.S. Department of Defense, Joint Publication 1 *Joint Warfare of the U.S. Armed Forces,* Washington, DC: U.S. Government Printing Office, November 11, 1991.

Joint Chiefs of Staff, U.S. Department of Defense, Joint Publication 5-0 *Joint Operation Planning,* Washington, DC: U.S. Government Printing Office, August 11, 2011.

New Zealand Defence Force, New Zealand Defence Doctrine Publication-Doctrine *Foundations of New Zealand Military Doctrine*, 1st ed., Wellington: Development Branch, Headquarters New Zealand Defence Force, 2004.

Prepared under the Direction of the Chief of the General Staff, *Design for Military Operations—British Military Doctrine,* London: Her Majesty's Stationary Office, 1989.

U.S. Air Force, Air Force Doctrine Document 1 *Air Force Basic Doctrine,* Maxwell Air Force Base: Headquarters Air Force Doctrine Centre, September 1997.

U.S. Army, FM 100-5 *Field Service Regulations: Operations* [first issued 1941]. Fort Leavenworth: U.S. Army Command and General Staff College Press, 1992.

UK Ministry of Defence, Joint Doctrine Publication 04 *Understanding,* Shrivenham, UK: Development Concepts and Doctrine Centre, December 2010.

Other Primary Sources

Australian Army, *Adaptive Campaigning: The Land Force Response to Complex Warfighting,* Version 4.18, reproduced as Appendix 2 to Scott Hopkins, ed., *Chief of Army's Exercise Proceedings 2006,* Duntroon: Australian Army Land Warfare Studies Centre, 2006, pp. 143–171.

Godefroy, Andrew B. ed., *Land Operations 2021: Adaptive Dispersed Operations—A Force Employment Concept for Canada's Army of Tomorrow,* Kingston, ON: Directorate of Land Concepts and Doctrine, 2007.

Krepinevich, Andrew F. *Why AirSea Battle?* Washington, DC: Center for Strategic and Budgetary Assessments, 2010.

Mattis, General J. N. *U.S. Joint Forces Command Commander's Guidance for Effects Based Operations,* unpublished memorandum dated 14 August 2008.

North Atlantic Treaty Organization, *NATO-Russia Glossary of Contemporary Political and Military Terms,* Brussels: NATO-Russia Joint Editorial Working Group, undated but promulgated online on June 8, 2001. Available from *www.nato.int/docu/glossary/eng/index.htm,* accessed on December 20, 2008.

PA Consulting Group, *Dynamic Planning for Counterinsurgency in Afghanistan,* PowerPoint Presentation, dated 2009, available from *http:// msnbcmedia.msn.com/i/MSNBC/Components/Photo/_new/ Afghanistan_ Dynamic_Planning.pdf,* accessed on May 1, 2012.

Tol, Jan van, with Mark Gunzinger, Andrew F. Krepinevich & Jim Thomas, *AirSea Battle: A Point of Departure Operational Concept,* Washington, DC: Centre for Strategic and Budgetary Assessments, 2010.

U.S. Army Combined Arms Center, "Doctrine Development", available from *http://usacac.army.mil/CAC/doctrine.asp,* accessed on August 8, 2010.

U.S. Department of Defense, *Sustaining U.S. Global Leadership: Priorities for 21st Century Defense,* Washington, DC: U.S. Government Printing Office, January 2012.

United Nations Department of Peacekeeping Operations, *United Nations Peacekeeping Operations: Principles and Guidelines,* New York, NY: United Nations, January 18, 2008.

United States Institute of Peace & U.S. Army Peacekeeping and Stability Operations Institute, *Guiding Principles for Stabilization and Reconstruction,* Washington, DC: United States Institute of Peace, 2009.

Secondary Sources

Books and Monographs

Alger, John A. *The Quest for Victory: The History of the Principles of War*, Contributions in Military History No. 30, Westport, CT: Greenwood Press, 1982.

Bacevich, A. J. *The Pentomic Era: The U.S. Army between Korea and Vietnam*, Washington, DC: National Defense University Press, 1986.

Bickerton, Ian, *The Illusion of Victory: The True costs of War,* Melbourne: Melbourne University Press, 2011.

Bonn, Kieth E. & Anthony E. Baker, *Guide to Military Operations Other Than War: Tactics, Techniques, and Procedures for Stability and Support Operations : Domestic and International*, Mechanicsburg PA: Stackpole Books, 2000.

Boot, Max, *The Savage Wars of Peace: Small Wars and the Rise of American Power*, New York: Basic Books, 2002.

Bousquet, Antoine, *The Scientific Way of Warfare: Order and Chaos on the Battlefields of Modernity,* London: Hurst and Co., 2009.

Brodie, Bernard, *War and Politics,* New York: MacMillan Publishing Co., 1973.

Builder Carl H. *The Masks of War: American Military Styles in Strategy and Analysis,* Baltimore MD: John Hopkins University Press, 1989.

Burrell, Gibson & Gareth Morgan, *Sociological Paradigms and Organisational Analysis: Elements of the Sociology of Corporate Life,* Portsmouth: Heinemenn, 1979.

Capra, Fritjof, *The Web of Life: A New Scientific Understanding of Living Systems,* New York, NY: Anchor Books, 1997.

Chapman, Bert, *Military Doctrine: A Reference Handbook,* Santa Barbara, CA: Praeger Security International, 2009.

Clausewitz, Carl von, *On War* [1832], edited and translated by Michael Howard and Peter Paret, Princeton NJ: Princeton University Press, 1989.

Clayton, Anthony, *The British Officer: Leading the Army from 1660 to the Present,* Edinburgh Gate: Pearson Education, 2007.

Cohen, Eliot A. *Supreme Command: Soldiers, Statesmen and Leadership in Wartime*, New York: The Free Press, 2002.

Crane, Conrad C. *Avoiding Vietnam: The U.S. Army's Response to Defeat in Southeast Asia,* Carlisle, PA: U.S. Army Strategic Studies Institute, September 2002.

Creveld, Martin van, *The Training of Officers: From Military Professionalism to Irrelevance*, New York, NY: The Free Press, 1990.

Davis II, Robert T. *The Challenge of Adaptation: The U.S. Army in the Aftermath of Conflict, 1953-2000,* Fort Leavenworth KS: Combat Studies Institute Press, March 2008.

Doughty, Robert A. *The Evolution of U.S. Army Tactical Doctrine, 1946-76*, Leavenworth Papers No. 1, Fort Leavenworth KS: Combat Studies Institute, August 1979.

Drew, Dennis M. & Donald M. Snow, *Making Strategy: An Introduction to National Security Processes and Problems*, Maxwell Air Force Base: Air University Press, 1988.

Echevarria II, Antulio J. *Rapid Decisive Operations: An Assumptions Based Critique*, Carlisle, PA: U.S. Army Strategic Studies Institute, November 2001.

Echevarria II, Antulio J. *Toward an American Way of War,* Carlisle: U.S. Army War College Strategic Studies Institute, March 2004.

Ellis, John, *The Social History of the Machine Gun*, London: Pimlico, 1976.

English, Allan D. *Understanding Military Culture: A Canadian Perspective,* Montreal, QC: McGill-Queens University Press, 2004.

Evans, Michael, *Forward from the Past: The Development of Australian Army Doctrine, 1972 – Present*, Study Paper No. 301, Canberra: Australian Army Land Warfare Studies Centre, August 1999.

Futrell, Robert, *Ideas, Concepts, Doctrine: Volume I: Basic Thinking in the United States Air Force 1907-1960,* Maxwell Air force Base: Air University Press, 1989.

Gat, Azar, *A History of Military Thought: From the Enlightenment to the Cold War,* Oxford: Oxford University Press, 2001.

Holden-Reid, Brian, *A Doctrinal Perspective: 1988-98*, Occasional Paper No. 33, United Kingdom: Strategic and Combat Studies Institute, May 1998.

Holsti, Kalevi J. *Peace and War: Armed Conflicts and International Order 1648-1989*, Cambridge Studies in International Relations No. 14, Cambridge: Cambridge University Press, 1991,

Huntington, Samuel P. *The Soldier and the State: The Theory and Politics of Civil-Military Relations*, Cambridge, MA: Harvard University Press, 1959.

Jackson, Aaron P. *Doctrine Development in Five Commonwealth Navies: A Comparative Perspective*, Papers in Australian Maritime Affairs No. 33, Canberra: Sea Power Centre—Australia, 2010.

Jackson, Aaron P. *Doctrine, Strategy and Military Culture: Military-Strategic Doctrine Development in Australia, Canada and New Zealand, 1987-2007,* Trenton, ON: Canadian Forces Aerospace Warfare Centre, 2013.

Jacob, Margaret C. *The Enlightenment: A Brief History with Documents,* Boston: Bedford/St Martins, 2001.

James, Glenn E. *Chaos Theory: The Essentials for Military Applications*, Newport Paper No. 10, Newport, RI: Naval War College, 1996.

Johnson, Phil & Joanne Duberley, *Understanding Management Research: An Introduction to Epistemology,* London: Sage Publications, 2000.

Kelly, Justin & Mike Brennan, *Alien: How Operational Art Devoured Strategy,* Carlisle, PA: U.S. Army Strategic Studies Institute, September 2009.

Krepinevich, Andrew F. *The Army and Vietnam,* Baltimore, MD: The John Hopkins University Press, 1986.

Kretchik, Walter E. *U.S. Army Doctrine: From the American Revolution to the War on Terror,* Lawrence, KS: University Press of Kansas, 2011.

Kuhn, Thomas S. *The Structure of Scientific Revolutions*, 3rd ed., Chicago, IL: Chicago University Press, 1996.

Leonhard, Robert R. *The Principles of War for the Information Age,* Novato, CA: Presidio, 1998.

Lock-Pullan, Richard, *U.S. Intervention Policy and Army Innovation: From Vietnam to Iraq,* New York, NY: Routledge, 2006.

Lynn, John A. *Battle: A History of Combat and Culture,* Cambridge, MA: Westview, 2003.

Mäder, Markus, *In Pursuit of Conceptual Excellence: The Evolution of British Military-Strategic Doctrine in the Post-Cold War Era, 1989- 2002,* Studies in Contemporary History and Security Policy No. 13, Bern: Peter Lang, 2004.

Mann, Michael, *The Sources of Social Power: Volume II: The Rise of Classes and Nation-States, 1760-1914,* Cambridge, UK: Cambridge University Press, 1993.

McAllister Linn, Brian, *The Echo of Battle: The Army's Way of War,* Cambridge, MA: Harvard University Press, 2007.

McNaugher, Thomas L. *Marksmanship, McNamara and the M16 Rifle: Organizations, Analysis and Weapons Acquisition,* RAND Paper No. P-6306, Santa Monica, CA: RAND Corporation, March 1979.

Middlemiss, Danford W. & Denis Stairs, *The Canadian Forces and the Doctrine of Interoperability: The Issues,* Policy Matters Occasional Paper Series, Vol. 3, No. 7, Montreal, QC: Institute for Research on Public Policy, June 2002.

Naveh, Shimon, *In Pursuit of Military Excellence: The Evolution of Operational Theory,* London: Frank Cass, 1997.

Okros, Alan, *Leadership in the Canadian Military Context,* Canadian Forces Leadership Institute Monograph 2010-01, Canada: Canadian Forces Leadership Institute, November 2010.

Osinga, Frans P. B. *Science, Strategy and War: The Strategic Theory of John Boyd,* London: Routledge, 2007.

Porter, Bruce D. *War and the Rise of the State: The Military Foundations of Modern Politics,* New York, NY: The Free Press, 1994.

Porter, Patrick, *Military Orientalism: Eastern War Through Western Eyes,* London: Hirst & Co, 2009.

Ricks, Thomas E. *The Gamble: General Petraeus and the Untold Story of the American Surge in Iraq, 2006-2008,* New York: Allen Lane, 2009.

Schneider, James J. *The Structure of Strategic Revolution: Total War and the Roots of the Soviet Warfare State,* Novato CA: Presidio Press, 1994.

Tilly, Charles, *Coercion, Capital, and European States, AD 990-1992,* Oxford: Blackwell, 1992.

Vego, Milan, *Joint Operational Warfare: Theory and Practice,* Newport RI: U.S. Naval War College, 2007.

Weigley, Russell F. *The American Way of War: A History of U.S. Military Strategy and Policy,* Bloomington, IN: Indiana University Press, 1973.

Westenhoff, Charles M. *Military Airpower: A Revised Digest of Airpower Opinions and Thoughts,* Maxwell Air Force Base: Air University Press, 2007.

Wight, Martin, *Systems of States,* Leicester, UK: Leicester University Press, 1977.

Williams, Michael, *Problems of Knowledge: A Critical Introduction to Epistemology,* Oxford: Oxford University Press, 2001.

Chapters in Edited Works

Bassford, Christopher, "Doctrinal Complexity: Nonlinearity in Marine Corps Doctrine," in F. G. Hoffman & Gary Horne, eds., *Maneuver Warfare Science 1998,* Washington DC: Department of the Navy, U.S. Marine Corps, 1998.

Black, Jeremy, "The Military Revolution II: Eighteenth-Century War," in Charles Townshend, ed., *The Oxford Illustrated History of Modern War,* Oxford: Oxford University Press, 1997.

Carver, Michael "Conventional Warfare in the Nuclear Age," in Peter Paret, ed., *Makers of Modern Strategy: From Machiavelli to the Nuclear Age,* Princeton, NJ: Princeton University Press, 1986.

Childs, John, "The Military Revolution I: The Transition to Modern Warfare," in Charles Townshend, ed., *The Oxford Illustrated History of Modern War,* Oxford: Oxford University Press, 1997.

Codner, Michael, "British Maritime Doctrine and National Military Strategy," in Centre for Defence Studies, Kings College London, *Brassey's Defence Yearbook 1996,* London: Brassey's, 1996.

Echevarria II, Antulio J. "American Operational Art, 1917-2008," in John Andreas Olsen & Martin van Creveld, *The Evolution of Operational Art: From Napoleon to the Present,* Oxford: Oxford University Press, 2011.

Comte, Auguste, "Plan of the Scientific Operations Necessary for Reorganizing Society" [1822]. Reproduced in: Lenzer, Gertrud, ed., *Auguste Comte and Positivism: The Essential Writings,* New York, NY: Harper & Row, 1975.

Gabel, Christopher R. "Preface," in U.S. Army, FM 100-5 *Field Service Regulations: Operations* [first issued 1941]. Fort Leavenworth: U.S. Army Command and General Staff College Press, 1992.

Gooch, John, "Introduction: Military Doctrine in Military History," in John Gooch, ed., *The Origins of Contemporary Doctrine*, Occasional Paper No. 30, Camberly: Strategic and Combat Studies Institute, September 1997.

Hattendorf, John B. "Introduction," in John B. Hattendorf, ed., *U.S. Naval Strategy in the 1990s: Selected Documents,* Newport Paper No. 27, Newport, RI: Naval War College Press, 2006.

Hayden, H. T. "Introduction: The History and Execution of Marine Corps Doctrine," in H. T. Hayden, ed., *Warfighting: Maneuver Warfare in the U.S. Marine Corps*, London: Greenhill Books, 1995.

Kipp, Jacob W. "The Tsarist and Soviet Operational Art, 1853-1991," in John Andreas Olsen & Martin van Creveld, *The Evolution of Operational Art: From Napoleon to the Present*, Oxford: Oxford University Press, 2011.

Klepak, Hal, "Some Reflections on Generalship Through the Ages," in Bernd Horn & Stephen J. Harris, eds., *Generalship and the Art of the Admiral: Perspectives on Canadian Senior Military Leadership,* St. Catherines, ON: Vanwell Publishing, 2001.

Langlois, Anthony J. "Human Rights," in Martin Griffiths, ed., *Encyclopedia of International Relations and Global Politics,* Abingdon: Routledge, 2006.

Makkreel, Rudolf, "Wilhelm Dilthey," in Edward N. Zalta, ed., *The Stanford Encyclopedia of Philosophy,* Summer 2012 edition, forthcoming. Available from *http://plato.stanford.edu/archives/ sum2012/entries/ dilthey/*, accessed on April 13, 2012.

Moller, P. Richard, "The Dangers of Doctrine," in *Maritime Security Working Paper No. 5,* Halifax: Dalhousie University, December 1996.

Moreman, Tim, "'The Greatest Training Ground in the World': The Army in India and the North-West Frontier, 1901-1947," in Daniel P. Marston & Chandar S. Sundaram, *A Military History of India and South Asia: From the East India Company to the Nuclear Era*, Bloomington, IN: Indiana University Press, 2008.

Romjue, John L. "The Evolution of American Army Doctrine," in John Gooch, ed., *The Origins of Contemporary Doctrine*, Occasional Paper No. 30, Camberly: Strategic and Combat Studies Institute, September 1997.

Sheffield, Gary, "Doctrine and Command in the British Army: An Historical Overview," in Directorate General Development and Doctrine, *Army Doctrine Publication: Land Operations,* United Kingdom: British Army, May 2005.

Showalter, Dennis E. "Prussian-German Operational Art, 1740-1943," in John Andreas Olsen & Martin van Creveld, *The Evolution of Operational Art: From Napoleon to the Present,* Oxford: Oxford University Press, 2011.

Shy, John, "Jomini," in Peter Paret, ed., *Makers of Modern Strategy: From Machiavelli to the Nuclear Age,* Princeton, NJ: Princeton University Press, 1986.

Spiller, Roger J. "In the Shadow of the Dragon: Doctrine and the U.S. Army after Vietnam," in Jeffrey Grey & Peter Dennis, eds., *From Past to Future: The Australian Experience of Land/Air Operations,* Canberra: Australian Defence Force Academy, 1995.

Strachan, Hew, "Operational Art in Britain, 1909-2009," in John Andreas Olsen & Martin van Creveld, *The Evolution of Operational Art: From Napoleon to the Present,* Oxford: Oxford University Press, 2011.

Weigley, Russell F. "American Strategy from its Beginnings through the First World War," in Peter Paret, ed., *Makers of Modern Strategy: From Machiavelli to the Nuclear Age,* Princeton, NJ: Princeton University Press, 1986.

Williams, John Allen, "The Postmodern Military Reconsdered," in Moskos, Charles C., John Allan Williams & David R. Segal, eds., *The Postmodern Military: Armed Forces after the Cold War,* New York, NY: Oxford University Press, 2000.

Edited Works

Centre for Defence Studies, Kings College London, *Brassey's Defence Yearbook 1996,* London: Brassey's, 1996.

Gooch, John, ed., *The Origins of Contemporary Doctrine,* Occasional Paper No. 30, Camberly: Strategic and Combat Studies Institute, September 1997.

Grey, Jeffrey & Peter Dennis, eds., *From Past to Future: The Australian Experience of Land/Air Operations,* Canberra: Australian Defence Force Academy, 1995.

Griffiths, Martin, ed., *Encyclopedia of International Relations and Global Politics,* Abingdon: Routledge, 2006.

Hattendorf, John B. ed., *U.S. Naval Strategy in the 1990s: Selected Documents,* Newport Paper No. 27, Newport, RI: Naval War College Press, 2006.

Hayden, H. T. ed., *Warfighting: Maneuver Warfare in the U.S. Marine Corps,* London: Greenhill Books, 1995.

Hoffman F. G. & Gary Horne, eds., *Maneuver Warfare Science 1998,* Washington DC: Department of the Navy, U.S. Marine Corps, 1998.

Horn, Bernd & Stephen J. Harris, eds., *Generalship and the Art of the Admiral: Perspectives on Canadian Senior Military Leadership,* St. Catharines, ON: Vanwell Publishing, 2001.

International Institute for Strategic Studies, "Complex Irregular Warfare: The Face of Contemporary Conflict," *The Military Balance,* Vol. 105, No. 1, 2005.

Lenzer, Gertrud, ed., *Auguste Comte and Positivism: The Essential Writings,* New York, NY: Harper & Row, 1975.

Marston, Daniel P. & Chandar S. Sundaram, *A Military History of India and South Asia: From the East India Company to the Nuclear Era,* Bloomington, IN: Indiana University Press, 2008.

Moskos, Charles C., John Allan Williams & David R. Segal, eds., *The Postmodern Military: Armed Forces after the Cold War,* New York, NY: Oxford University Press, 2000.

Olsen, John Andreas & Martin van Creveld, *The Evolution of Operational Art: From Napoleon to the Present,* Oxford: Oxford University Press, 2011.

Paret, Peter, ed., *Makers of Modern Strategy: From Machiavelli to the Nuclear Age,* Princeton, NJ: Princeton University Press, 1986.

Townshend, Charles ed., *The Oxford Illustrated History of Modern War,* Oxford: Oxford University Press, 1997.

Journal Articles

Banach Stefan J. & Alex Ryan, "The Art of Design: A Design Methodology," *Military Review,* Vol. 89, No. 2, March/April 2009, pp. 105-115.

Bullock, Xander & Bruce Vitor, "Design: How, Not Why," *Military Review,* Vol. 90. No. 2, March/April 2010, pp. 102-108.

Cardon Edward C. & Steve Leonard, "Unleashing Design: Planning and the Art of Battle Command," *Military Review,* Vol. 90, No. 2, March/ April 2010, pp. 2-12.

Cebrowski Arthur K. & John J. Garstka, "Network-Centric Warfare: Its Origin and Future," *Proceedings*, Vol. 124, No. 1, January 1998, pp. 28-35.

Clay, John S. "The Fifth Service Looks at Doctrine," *Joint Force Quarterly*, No. 14, Winter 1996-7, pp. 29-33.

Codner, Michael, "Purple Prose and Purple Passion: The Joint Defence Centre," *RUSI Journal*, Vol. 144, No. 1, February/March 1999, pp. 36-40.

Coffman, Edward M. "The Long Shadow of *The Soldier and the State*," *Journal of Military History*, Vol. 55, No. 1, January 1991, pp. 69-82.

Cook, Martin L. "Revolt of the Generals: A Case Study in Professional Ethics," *Parameters*, Vol. XXXVIII, No. 1, pp. 4-15.

Coombs, Howard G. "In the Wake of a Paradigm Shift: The Canadian Forces College and the Operational Level of War (1987-1995)," *Canadian Military Journal*, Vol. 10 No. 2, 2010, pp. 19-27.

Cox, David & Andrew O'Neil, "Professional Military Education in Australia: Has it All Gone Terribly Right?" *Australian Defence Force Journal*, No. 171, 2006, pp. 57-74.

Davidson, Ketti, "From Tactical Planning to Operational Design," *Military Review*, Vol. 88, No. 5, September/October 2008, pp. 33-39.

Elkus, Adam & Crispin Burke, "Operational Design: Promise and Problems," *Small Wars Journal*, February 2010. Available from *http:// smallwarsjournal.com/blog/journal/docs-temp/362-elkus.pdf*, accessed on April 16, 2012.

Elkus, Adam, "Complexity, Design, and Modern Operational Art: U.S. Evolution or False Start?" *Canadian Army Journal*, Vol. 13, No. 3, Autumn 2010, pp. 55-67.

Evans, Michael, "From Kadesh to Kandahar: Military Theory and the Future of War," *Naval War College Review*, Vol. LVI, No. 3, Summer 2003, pp. 132-150.

Feld, M. D. "Middle-Class Society and the Rise of Military Professionalism: The Dutch Army 1589-1609," *Armed Forces and Society*, Vol. 1, No. 4, August 1975, pp. 419-442.

Goddard, David, "Max Weber and the Objectivity of Social Science," *History and Theory*, Vol. 12, No. 1, 1973, pp. 1-22.

Gray, Colin S. "Concept Failure: COIN, Counterinsurgency, and Strategic Theory," *Prism*, Vol. 3, No. 3, June 2012, pp. 17-32.

Greenwood T. C. & T. X. Hammes, "War Planning for Wicked Problems: Where Joint Doctrine Fails," *Armed Forces Journal*, December 2009, available from *www.armedforcesjournal.com/2009/12/4252237*, accessed on April 16, 2012.

Haas, Peter, "Introduction: Epistemic Communities and International Policy Coordination," *International Organization*, Vol. 46, No. 1, Winter 1992, pp. 1-35.

Jablonsky, David, "U.S. Military Doctrine and the Revolution in Military Affairs," *Parameters*, Vol. 24, No. 3, Autumn 1994, pp. 18-36.

Jackson, Aaron P. "Getting it Right? Military-Strategic Level Doctrine Development in New Zealand," *New Zealand Journal of Defence Studies*, Vol. 3, August 2008, pp. 11-17.

Jackson, Aaron P. "Moving Beyond Manoeuvre: A Conceptual Coming- of-age for the Australian and Canadian Armies," *Australian Defence Force Journal*, No. 177, November/December 2008, pp. 85-100.

Jackson, Aaron P. "The Emergence of a "Doctrinal Culture" within the Canadian Air Force: Where it Came From, Where it's at and Where to From Here? Part One: Doctrine and Canadian Air Force Culture Prior to the End of the Cold War," *Canadian Air Force Journal*, Vol. 2, No. 3, Summer 2009, pp. 38-46.

Johnston, Paul, "Doctrine is not Enough: The Effect of Doctrine on the Behavior of Armies," *Parameters*, Vol. XXX, No. 3, Autumn 2000, pp. 30-39.

Kaplan, Fred, "The End of the Age of Petraeus: The Rise and Fall of Counterinsurgency," *Foreign Affairs*, Vol. 92, No. 1, January/ February 2013, pp. 75-90.

Krauthammer, Charles, "The Unipolar Moment," *Foreign Affairs*, Vol. 70, No. 1, Winter 1990-1, pp. 23-33.

Lauder, Matthew, "Systemic Operational Design: Freeing Operational Planning from the Shackles of Linearity," *Canadian Military Journal*, Vol. 9, No. 4, 2009, pp. 41-49.

Locher, James R. "Has it Worked? The Goldwater-Nichols Reorganization Act," *Naval War College Review*, Vol. LIV, No. 4, Autumn 2001, pp. 95-115.

Lock-Pullan, Richard, "How to Rethink War: Conceptual Innovation and AirLand Battle Doctrine," *Journal of Strategic Studies*, Vol. 28, No. 4, August 2005, pp. 679-702.

Mann, Steven R. "Chaos Theory and Strategic Thought," *Parameters*, Vol. XXII, No. 3, Autumn 1992, pp. 54-68.

McMaster, H. R. "On War: Lessons to be Learned," *Survival*, Vol. 50, No. 1, February-March 2008, pp. 19-30.

Mitchell, Paul T. "EBO: Thinking Effects and Effective Thinking," *Pointer*, Vol. 33, No. 1, 2007, pp. 50-58.

Owen, William F. "Essay: The War of New Words: Why Military History Trumps Buzzwords," *Armed Forces Journal*, November 2009, available from *www.armedforcesjournal.com/2009/11/4114043*, accessed on April 17, 2012.

Paparone, Christopher R. "Design and the Prospects for Decision," *Small Wars Journal*, November 2010, available online from *http://smallwarsjournal.com/blog/journal/docs-temp/598-paparone.pdf*, accessed October 2, 2012.

Paparone, Christopher R. "FM 3-0: Operations on the Cusp of Postpositivism," *Small Wars Journal*, May 2008, available from *http://smallwarsjournal.com/blog/journal/docs-temp/65-paparone.pdf*, accessed on February 17, 2011.

Perez Jr., Celestino, "A Practical Guide to Design: A Way to Think About It, and A Way to Do It," *Military Review*, Vol. 91, No. 2, March/April 2011, pp. 41-51.

Romjue, John L. "The Evolution of the AirLand Battle Concept," *Air University Review*, May-June 1984. Available from *www.airpower.maxwell.af.mil/airchronicles/aureview/1984/may-jun/romjue.html*, accessed on November 30, 2009.

Rotmann, Philipp, David Tohn & Jaron Wharton, "Learning Under Fire: Progress and Dissent in the U.S. Military," *Survival*, Vol. 54, No. 1, August-September 2009, pp. 31-48.

Schaefer, Christof, "Design: Extending Military Relevance," *Military Review*, Vol. 89, No. 5, September/October 2009, pp. 29-39.

Taw, Jennifer Morrison, "Stability and Support Operations: History and Debates," *Studies in Conflict and Terrorism*, Vol. 33, No. 5, 2010, pp. 387-407.

Taylor, R. K. "2020 Vision: Canadian Forces Operational-Level Doctrine," *Canadian Military Journal*, Vol. 2, No. 3, Autumn 2001, pp. 35-42.

Thomas George M. & John W. Meyer, "The Expansion of the State," *Annual Review of Sociology*, No. 10, 1984, pp. 461-482.

Tritten, James J. "Developing Naval Doctrine ...*From the Sea,*" *Joint Force Quarterly*, No. 9, Autumn 1995, pp. 110-113.

Vego, Milan N. "A Case Against Systemic Operational Design," *Joint Force Quarterly*, No. 53, 2nd Quarter 2009, pp. 69-75.

Vohr, J Alex, "Design in the Context of Operational Art," *Marine Corps Gazette*, Vol. 94, No. 1, January 2010, pp. 39-42.

Walker, David L. "Refining the Military Appreciation Process for Adaptive Campaigning," *Australian Army Journal*, Vol. 8, No. 2, Winter 2011, pp. 85-100.

Wass de Czege, Huba, "Systemic Operational Design: Learning and Adapting in Complex Missions," *Military Review*, Vol. 89, No. 1, January/February 2009, pp. 2-12.

Yingling, Paul, "A Failure in Generalship," *Armed Forces Journal*, May 2007, available from *www.armedforcesjournal.com/2007/05/2635198*, accessed on October 28, 2009.

Other Secondary Sources

Berlow, Eric, *How Complexity Leads to Simplicity,* TED: Talks in Less Than Six Minutes, July 2010, available from *www.ted.com/talks/eric_berlow_how_complexity_leads_to_simplicity.html*, accessed on May 15, 2012.

Maltz, Richard, "The Epistemology of Strategy," paper presented at the XX Annual Strategy Conference, U.S. Army War College, Carlisle PA, April 17, 2009.

Nagl, John "The Evolution and Importance of Army/Marine Corps Field Manual 3-24, Counterinsurgency," *Small Wars Journal* Blog Post, June 27, 2007, available from *http://smallwarsjournal.com/blog/the-evolution-and-importance-of-armymarine-corps-field-manual-3-24-counterinsurgency*, accessed on April 5, 2012.

Nort, Richard M. van, *The Battle of Adrianople and the Military Doctrine of Vegitius,* The City University of New York: Unpublished PhD Dissertation, 2007.

Schamburg, Gary R. *Cloud Patterns: An Operational Hierarchy?* Unpublished monograph, Fort Leavenworth, KS: School of Advanced Military Studies, Academic Year 1994-5.

Sheets, Thomas E. *"Training" and "Educating" Marine Corps Officers for the Future*, unpublished monograph: U.S. Army War College, April 1992, available from *http://www.dtic.mil/dtic/tr/fulltext/u2/a249432.pdf*, accessed on September 30, 2012.

Sorrels, William T., Glen R. Downing, Paul J. Blakesley, David W. Pendall, Jason K. Walk & Richard D. Wallwork, *Systemic Operational Design: An Introduction*, unpublished monograph: School of Advanced Military Studies, U.S. Army Command and General Staff College, academic year 2004-5, available from *www.dtic.mil/cgi-bin/ GetTRDoc?AD=ADA479311*, accessed on April 11, 2012.

Stofka, Jonathan M. *Designing the Desired State: A Process and Model for Operational Design*, unpublished Masters thesis: Marine Corps University Command and Staff College, academic year 2009-10, available from

www.mcu.usmc.mil/Student%20Research/STOFKA%20-%20 MMS%20Paper%20AY%202010.pdf, accessed on April 10, 2012.

Author Biography

Dr Aaron P. Jackson is a Doctrine Desk Officer at the Australian Defence Force (ADF) Joint Doctrine Centre. In this appointment he has been project manager and/or lead author of six doctrine publications, including Australian Defence Doctrine Publication (ADDP) 00.1—*Command and Control*, edition 2, and ADDP 5.0—*Joint Planning*, edition 2. He has also contributed in various ways during the development of fifteen other joint doctrine and related publications, including interagency projects such as the *Guide to Defence and Australian Federal Police (International Deployment Group) Interoperability for Offshore Operations*, for which he was the ADF's primary representative and key content authority, and a contributing author. Aaron has also served in the Australian Army Reserve for over ten years. He has deployed on operations in Timor Leste and has served on exercise or exchange in the United States, New Zealand and the Philippines. He holds a Doctorate of Philosophy (International Relations) and is appointed as a Visiting Fellow at the Griffith Asia Institute, Griffith University, Australia. He is the author of *Doctrine, Strategy and Military Culture: Military-Strategic Doctrine Development in Australia, Canada and New Zealand, 1987-2007* (Canadian Forces Aerospace Warfare Centre, 2013), *Keystone Doctrine Development in Five Commonwealth Navies: A Comparative Perspective* (Sea Power Centre-Australia, 2010), and several peer-reviewed journal articles and other academic papers.

Author's note: My thanks to Drs Alan Okros and Eric Oullet, and to Colonel Howard Coombs PhD, for their valuable feedback on earlier drafts. I would also like to offer a special thank you to Dr Paul T. Mitchell, who volunteered a lot of his time to act as an unofficial mentor to me during the development of this monograph. Any errors are, of course, my own.